FAMI

ULSTER GENEALOG

Ulster
Genealogical
& Historical
Guild

NUMBER 17

2001

INCORPORATING ULSTER GENEALOGICAL & HISTORICAL GUILD NEWSLETTER

Front cover: Beatty's Entry, 1912, BEL 102, reproduced with the kind permission of the Trustees of MAGNI (Ulster Museum). The household return of the MacKinnon family, 1901 Census, County Antrim. MIC 354/1/14, reproduced by kind permission of PRONI.

Back cover: Restaurant staff of the Grand Central Hotel, Belfast, 1936 H10/21/1014, reproduced with the kind permission of the Trustees of MAGNI (Ulster Museum). Ulster Volunteer Force drilling, *c* 1913, YOUNG D. 3027, reproduced by kind permission of PRONI.

First published 2001
by the Ulster Historical Foundation
12 College Square East, Belfast BT1 6DD
www.ancestryireland.com

ISBN 1-903688-16-7

Cover design by Dunbar Design
Printed by ColourBooks Limited, Dublin

CONTENTS

EDITORIAL

The current issue of *Familia: Ulster Genealogical Review* includes contributions from Ireland north and south, Great Britain, Australia, South Africa and the United States, a reflection of the breadth of interests and geographical locations of our readership. The emphasis, as has been the case now for a number of years, is on the telling of a good story and the availability of sources that were consulted in the research, all with a view to being ultimately useful and accessible to a wider audience.

There have been few sources whose unavailability in Ireland has been lamented more than the decennial census records from 1821. All nineteenth-century census records have long been destroyed as a result of official misguidedness or as victims of the Troubles of the early 1920s that accompanied the partitioning of Ireland. We have long envied our counterparts in Great Britain their access to these census records. On the other hand, the availability of the 1901 and 1911 census enumerators' returns in Dublin has been something of a remedial bonus. The articles by Brenda Collins (on the research value evident in twentieth-century Irish census records) and Margaret Brennand (on the forthcoming availability of the 1901 census records for England and Wales at the Public Record Office at Kew, where the resourceful provision of the new technology should facilitate access on a greater scale than ever before bring readers up to date. In this regard at least the release of the 1901 census records at Kew could well become a landmark in the development of electronic access to what has become a staple source for historian and genealogist alike.

Information on new sources is very much a feature of Richard McMaster's account of the business records of James Fullton, an eighteenth-century Philadelphia merchant, which outline the extent of transatlantic mercantile and passenger traffic (an aspect which features in Brenda Collins's review of the publication of Thomas Greg and Waddell Cunningham's letter book 1756-7). Trevor McClaughlin's research on the records of the judiciary in Victoria and New South Wales has provided fresh insights not only on the role of Irish women migrants to colonial Australia but also on how society judged them in more senses than one. Leslie McCracken's account of the Porter family over the generations from c.1800 reflects on the bicentenary of the coming into effect of the Act of Union between Great Britain and Ireland. The coming into operation of the Government of Northern Ireland eighty years ago is marked by Sir Kenneth Bloomfield's biographical accounts of the respective heads of its civil service 1921-2001. My former colleague in the Public Record Office of Northern Ireland Ian Montgomery's account of the struggle relating to access of another kind, right of way to the Giant's Causeway, Ulster's most popular visitor attraction, is an issue which continues even as this publication is going to press. Who says we have nothing to learn from history?

Trevor Parkhill
Keeper of History
Ulster Museum

NOTES ON CONTRIBUTORS

Sir Kenneth Bloomfield is a former Head of the Northern Ireland Civil Service who has recently published a study of victims of the Northern Ireland Troubles, he is also a Trustee of UHF.

Brenda Collins is Research Officer at the Irish Linen Centre, Lisburn Museum.

Margaret Brennand is Communications Co-ordinator of the 1901 Census Project in the Public Record Office, Kew.

Trevor McClaughlin is Reader in History, Macquarie University, Sydney, Australia.

Leslie McCracken is a former professor of history in the New University of Ulster, later University of Ulster, now living in South Africa.

Richard McMaster has recently retired as professor of history, Bluffton College, Ohio and now lives in Florida.

Ian Montgomery, sometime Archivist in PRONI and Belfast City Council, is Researcher & Historian at Muckamore Abbey Hospital, Co. Antrim.

Bill Crawford, formerly of PRONI and the Ulster Folk & Transport Museum, is Vice-Chairman of UHF.

Bill Maguire is a former Head of the Division of Human History of the Ulster Museum and recently retired Chairman of the Board of Irish Historical Studies.

Anita Gallagher is Project Officer with the Border Counties History Collective based at Blacklion in Co. Cavan.

Jane Williams, a graduate of Cambridge University, is History Education Officer in the Ulster Museum/MAGNI.

Trevor Parkhill is Keeper of History in the Ulster Museum/MAGNI and Editor of *Familia*.

Five generations of the MacKinnon family of Cloughcorr in 1901.
From left: Mary J. Donnelly (daughter); on her lap, John Alexander MacKinnon Donnelly (great-great-grandson); John Donnelly (grandson); James A. Donnelly (great-grandson); Alexander MacKinnon (head of family) born 1799, d. 1903.

See 1901 Census Household return of MacKinnon family, p.7.

BEEN THERE, DONE THAT: THE AVAILABILITY AND USES OF IRISH TWENTIETH CENTURY CENSUS RECORDS

Brenda Collins

Original census returns, on household forms, generally completed by the head of the household, constitute one of the building blocks of primary material for the study of history in the nineteenth century and later. Within the British Isles, censuses organised by the state were undertaken every ten years between 1801 and 1911. Within Scotland and in Ireland the census administration was undertaken by the relevant government departments which is why the survival of the original enumeration information of the household returns and the access to these valuable records has been by no means uniform throughout the British Isles.[1]

Since the 1960s there has been in Britain a steadily growing interest in the use of the census enumeration books from the 1841 and subsequent censuses. Although much of the interest has originated with genealogists, it has built on and itself contributed to the growth of interest in local studies and the foundation of local historical societies, as well as providing additions to scholarship and debates on wider concerns of social and economic history. The implementation, in England and Wales, of a '100 year rule' for reasons of discretion in revealing personal data has meant that, at successive ten yearly intervals, a vast source of historical information has been made available. Indeed, alongside the increase in interest in the use of census material, access arrangements have had to be more rigidly enforced. The account given by Margaret Brennand later in this journal, of the efforts that the Public Record Office at Kew has taken to make more widely available than ever before the 1901 census for England and Wales from 1 January 2002, will certainly be good news for searchers with an interest in this source and who may have been mindful of the inconsistencies in their availability compared with the picture in Ireland. In Scotland, of course, as in Ireland the '100 year rule' on closure of the census schedules was not applied, with the result that all of the surviving nineteenth century censuses have been open for research since the 1970s.

Within Irish archives administration, the acknowledgement of the limited quantity of surviving material seems to have had a significant effect on the issue of access. Firstly, in contrast to the position in Great Britain there was, in Ireland, the destruction of the vast majority of the manuscript material collected in connection with the decennial censuses. The census schedules from the 1861-1891 censuses were destroyed by government order during the First World War; those from the censuses prior to, and including, 1851 were largely lost in the fire and destruction of the Four Courts building during the War of Independence in 1922. Any visitor to the National Archives in Dublin who has experienced a chilling, yet poignant, brush with the conflagration through having requested a document which appears to have charred edges gains an immediate understanding of the phrase 'chance historical survival'. Still, because, or in spite, of this paucity of nineteenth-century data, the census schedules of 1901 and 1911 for the entire island of Ireland are available for study in the National Archives in Dublin with microfilm copies available elsewhere, most notably at PRONI which holds microfilm copies of the 1901 census for the six counties of Northern Ireland.

People who study the census returns do so principally for personal or professional interests. They may be either genealogists in dogged pursuit of the last piece of the jigsaw of ancestry or they may have a passing interest; others have a wider focus either in local history through studying a community or a group of people such as mill workers; yet others study the census enumeration material in order to repackage that information into other themes of interest such as the quality of housing or social class differences. The primacy of the census enumeration as a source document is that, by virtue of its standardisation of information about individuals, it stands centrally at the interchange between personal biography and general history; census records provide the fulcrum between the personal, local and unique phenomena and the general, national and aggregated evidence. The 1901 census, as the first census of the twentieth century, just missed being part of the Victorian era by a few months. By the time of the next census, in 1911, the Edwardian period had ended and George V was on the throne. In terms of British history, that pre-First World War period is viewed as something of an Indian summer. During that period there was, however, the beginning of increased active state intervention in welfare, health and pension provision, all of which attempted to deal with the aspects of early twentieth-century society revealed by the census.

Throughout the British Isles, the 1901 census was taken on the night of Sunday 30 March and the 1911 census on the night of Sunday 2 April. As the full purpose of a census is to record a snapshot view at a point of time, all households were visited by a census enumerator in the following days who required the household head to recall and record who had resided in the household on census night. For the 1901 enumeration in Ireland, the country was divided into 208 enumeration districts with a total number of 3941 temporary enumerators. The enumerators were all members of the Royal Irish Constabulary, or, in Dublin, members of the Dublin Metropolitan Police. The role of the police in the census enumeration had been established, in Ireland, in the 1841 census enumeration, as also was the townland as a territorial unit of classification: both facets of the 1841 census administration made use of the recently established examples of the local application of Irish public administration centred in Dublin, the Constabulary and the Ordnance Survey six-inch mapping of Ireland. In England and Wales, where civil registration had been introduced in 1836, the local census administration was based on the civil registration districts and organized by the registrars, while Scotland adopted the same procedures after the introduction of civil registration in 1855. Presumably, by 1864, when comprehensive civil registration was established in Ireland, the local administrative system that had been so efficient in the management of the three previous censuses was considered to have proved its worth and so the temporary deployment of the constabulary continued.[2]

The administration and classification of the 1901 and the 1911 census enumeration material and the published reports have a common and complex referencing system which had, at its most specific level of data collation, the townland. The Poor Law Union Act of 1838 had established workhouse admission procedures and entitlements to dispensary treatment based on Poor Law Union areas which were divided into Dispensary Districts based on Electoral Divisions of groups of townlands. When civil registration was introduced in 1864, the separate hierarchy of Superintendent Registration Districts and Registration Districts was generally coterminous with the Poor Law Unions and the Dispensary Districts. The 1898 Local Government (Ireland) Act continued the use of the same District Electoral Divisions for elective rural and urban district councils and hence the 1901 census enumeration districts were the groups of townlands which made up the District Electoral Divisions (DEDs). Prior to the nineteenth century, Ireland's local administrative framework had been defined in terms of baronies and civil parishes and, though their functions as administrative units were largely abandoned, their definitions were retained for reference purposes in the indexes and published census reports.

Townlands thus form the organising principle behind the administrative classifications. A valuable supplement to the 1901 and 1911 censuses (and one which was also published in relation to the 1851 and 1871 censuses) is the 1901 Alphabetical Index to the Townlands, Towns, Parishes, and Baronies of Ireland, which supplies the name and number of the DED in which a townland is situated. Each DED has the same sequential number in the published census reports and in the National Archives classification of its enumeration returns.

The sheer number of townlands, over 64,000 in 1901, some with very few inhabitants, precluded the publication of any detailed statistics at this level, and only the basic population totals and numbers of houses are given in the census reports. However, the grouping of townlands into DEDs, Registration Districts and Dispensary Districts opens up a much wider range of information on issues such as age structures and literacy levels.

By the 1901 census, in the cities of Dublin, Cork, Limerick, Galway, Belfast and Derry, of course, townlands as a basis for organisation were superseded by political wards. However, the townland groupings continued to be used in all smaller towns and villages. Thus the household returns of each townland, or street in a town, are grouped together. Each townland's returns are arranged in alphabetical order within each DED, as they are in the published census reports. Indexes are available on this basis for each county.

To anyone familiar with the census enumeration books of England, Scotland and Wales, there is an immediate difference in the Irish material because the enumerators recorded no information regarding the extent or sequence of the route which they undertook in visiting the houses. However, the boundaries of townlands may be clarified by the study of an Ordnance Survey map, the specific references for which accompany the townland entry in the Topographical Index, while in towns the locations of streets can be obtained from large scale town plans and directories.

The range of data collected by the census enumerators is both wide and uniform throughout the country. Its scope as a source therefore raises an immense variety of information about households and people while the method of its operation means that each set of household returns of a townland or street can be compared with its immediate neighbour or even a household on the other side of the country.

Each household return is on Form A. In contrast to the census enumeration in Great Britain which is preserved in the form of the census enumeration books into which the enumerators copied their household forms, in Ireland it is the original schedules which have been preserved and microfilmed.

From the viewpoint of authenticity, therefore, what has been preserved in Ireland is less likely to have been subject to transcription errors than the material in Great Britain. The personal information comprises (commencing with the head), the name and surname of each household member, their relationship to the household head, their religious denomination, level of literacy in English, age, gender, occupation, marital status, county of birth (if in Ireland, or, if elsewhere, the country), ability to speak Irish, and disabilities, if any. In the 1911 census throughout the British Isles, information was also requested on years of marriage, and numbers of children born and surviving. The interest in such questions arose from the general awareness of the decline in family size which had been observed to have taken place at the end of the nineteenth century.

An example of a household return from the 1901 census of Ireland is reproduced in Fig. 1. This is a household in the townland of Cloghcorr, near Ballintoy, County Antrim. The household head on census night was listed as Alexander MacKinnon, a widower farmer, aged 101 years. Also resident in the household was his son, 65 year old James Francis MacKinnon, a civil engineer by profession. Two female domestic servants and the young daughter of one of them also were present and the younger of the two servants had been born in America. All the others were born either in Cloghcorr (the MacKinnons) or in nearby townlands. The richness of this detailed personal information is heightened by the family photograph of the MacKinnons, reproduced as a frontispiece on p. vi. This photograph, also taken in 1901, by a professional photographer, Lee,[3] was clearly intended as a record for posterity and shows old Alexander, on the right, with his daughter, Mary J. Donnelly, holding Alexander's great-great-grandson, John Alexander MacKinnon, on her knee. Behind them stand John Donnelly, Alexander's grandson and James A. Donnelly, Alexander's great-grandson. The birthdates of this family portrait span an extraordinary 102 years. The statutory preservation of the census and the family's regard for their historical record enables the twenty-first century researcher to see and appreciate, Alexander MacKinnon, himself born in the eighteenth century.

In addition to the personal information on Form A there is also information on all the occupied houses which is presented on several summary forms at the beginning of each townland or street. Form B1, for example, provides the name of the landholder of the property. In addition, it includes evaluative criteria for the standard of the housing, namely the construction materials of walls and roof and the number of windows and of rooms at the front of the house. By these standards, set by the Census Commissioners, the Mackinnons occupied a '1st class' house, stone-built, with eight rooms and nine windows on the front. On a subsequent form, B2, a count is given of the number and type of the outbuildings of each property while Form N provides an abstract of the gender, religious denomination and total number of people in each enumerated household and in the entire set.

From Form B2 we learn that the MacKinnon household had sixteen outhouses in all, including a coach house, two stables, as well as sheds for cows, calves, pigs, fowl and potatoes.

The case of the MacKinnon household demonstrates the contribution that the study of census material in combination with photographic documentation can make to a local historical study. The study of rural housing, for example, can be fully documented throughout the 1901 census 'snapshot', an impossibility in Great Britain where no similar details of housing conditions were collected. This numeric classification of housing, first used in the 1841 census of Ireland, was a concept ahead of its time in its assignment of quantitative codes to qualitative characteristics. This enabled an aggregated rank order to be established into which houses could be placed.[4]

Census schedules can also be used in conjunction with folk memory recollections, either written down or collected orally. Mawhinney used such a locally-published autobiography to augment a census analysis of houses and families in Owenreagh, County Londonderry. This

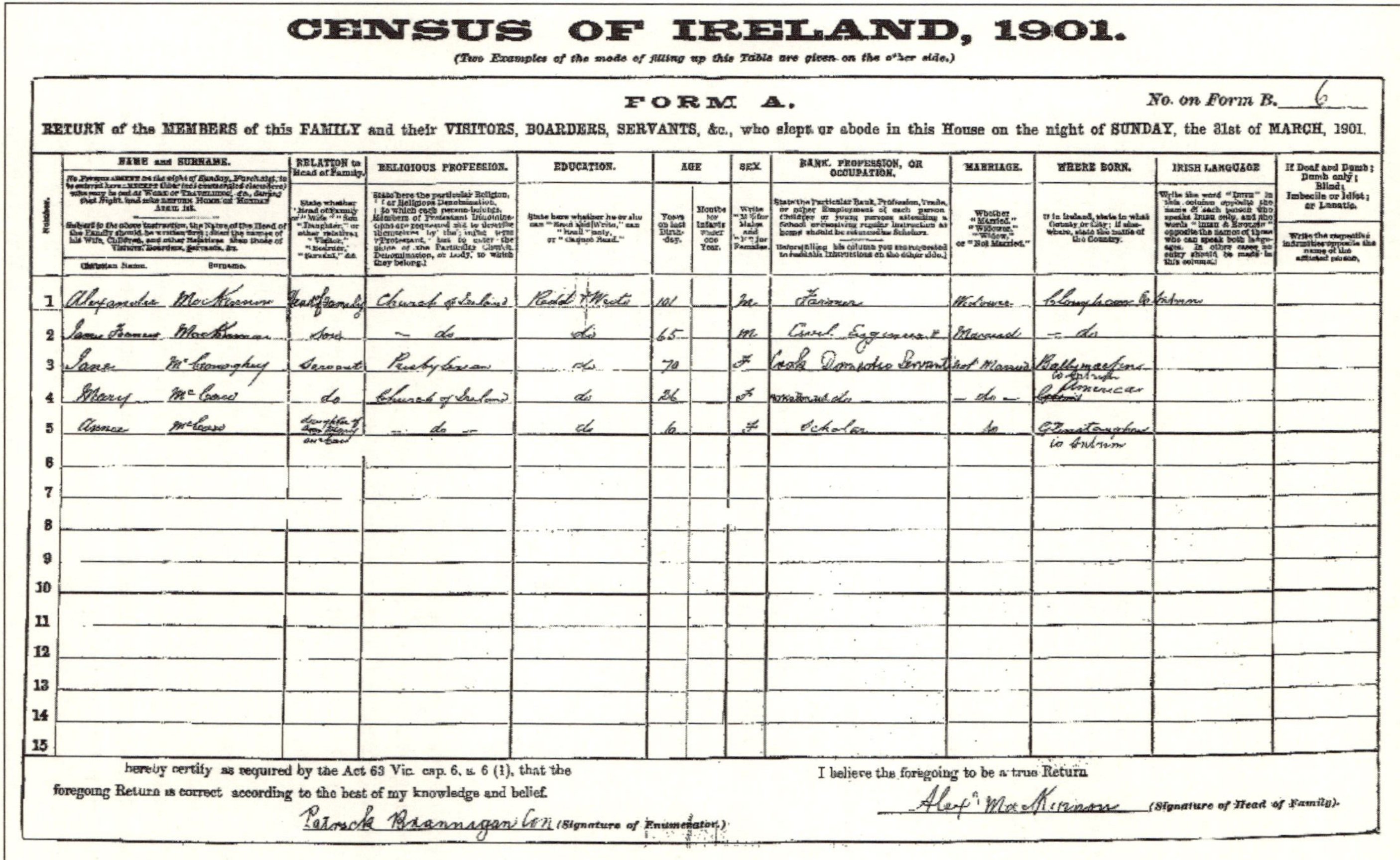

CENSUS OF IRELAND, 1901.

(Two Examples of the mode of filling up this Table are given on the other side.)

FORM A. No. on Form B. 6

RETURN of the MEMBERS of this FAMILY and their VISITORS, BOARDERS, SERVANTS, &c., who slept or abode in this House on the night of SUNDAY, the 31st of MARCH, 1901.

Number	Christian Name	Surname	Relation to Head of Family	Religious Profession	Education	Age (Years on last Birthday)	Age (Months for Infants under one Year)	Sex	Rank, Profession, or Occupation	Marriage	Where Born	Irish Language	If Deaf and Dumb; Dumb only; Blind; Imbecile or Idiot; or Lunatic
1	Alexander	MacKinnon	Head of Family	Church of Ireland	Read & Write	101		M	Farmer	Widower	Cloughcorr Co Antrim		
2	James Francis	MacKinnon	Son	– do	do	65		M	Civil Engineer	Married	– do		
3	Jane	McConaghy	Servant	Presbyterian	do	70		F	Cook Domestic Servant	Not Married	Ballymacfine Co Antrim		
4	Mary	McCann	do	Church of Ireland	do	36		F	Waitress do	– do –	American Colonies		
5	Anna	McCann	daughter of Mary McCann	– do –	do	6		F	Scholar	do	Glenstaughey Co Antrim		
6													
7													
8													
9													
10													
11													
12													
13													
14													
15													

I hereby certify as required by the Act 63 Vic. cap. 6, s. 6 (1), that the foregoing Return is correct according to the best of my knowledge and belief.

Patrick Brannigan Con (Signature of Enumerator.)

I believe the foregoing to be a true Return.

Alexr MacKinnon (Signature of Head of Family).

Household return of MacKinnon family, 1901 Census, County Antrim. Mic 354/1/14. Ballintoy DED, Cloughcorr townland. Reproduced by kind permission of PRONI description of turn of the twentieth century housing interior would not have been so very different to that of the MacKinnons.

> The dwelling house was of two storeys, built of stone, rough cast on the outside with lime mortar and whitewashed and it had a slate roof. There was a large kitchen-living room, a parlour (not much used), three bedrooms and a fairly big pantry. Some rooms were papered, others plastered smooth and whitewashed... There were two fireplaces, a large open fireplace in the kitchen and a small grate in the parlour...The kitchen fire never went out. At night it was banked up and in the morning it was raked out and it was still burning brightly.[5]

Where the MacKinnon household represented generations of settled farm ownership, a photograph in the Green Collection at the Ulster Folk & Transport Museum (see p. 9) depicts the much more humble way of life of a family in Gortnamoney townland, on the outskirts of Moira, County Down. The woman sitting sewing outside the cottage was enumerated in the 1901 census as Isabella McCoy, then aged 18 years old. She lived with her mother, Elizabeth, aged 53, and her 19-year-old brother, James. Both mother and son were listed by the census enumerator as damask weavers. Elizabeth was unable to write her signature on the census form, which was completed by the enumerator on her behalf. However, the summary table, Form N, has James the son, listed as household head, even though his mother, Elizabeth, is clearly first on the census form. Bella McCoy was a seamstress and the photograph shows clearly her drawn-thread needlework skills. Small table cloths such as the one illustrated (used at supper or breakfast) were ornamented and stitched by women and girls working at home with materials supplied by local linen weaving companies.[6] By the early twentieth century, both sewing outwork and damask weaving were paid at very low rates, though the products were exported all over the world as quality Irish linen. The McCoys' four-roomed cottage is still standing, though now derelict.

A community such as the families living in the rural area between Moira, Lurgan and Portadown in north-west County Down has been studied by Crawford using the 1901 census.[7] His analysis of the population change in the townlands of Bleary, Ballydugan and Clare uses the aggregate statistics and the household composition revealed in the census enumeration schedules. The predominant means of earning a living was through textiles worked at home; damask and

Isabella McCoy (seated), with her drawn-thread needlework, outside the family cottage.
From the Green Collection (WAG286) Ulster Folk & Transport Museum.
Reproduced by kind permission of the Trustees, MAGNI.

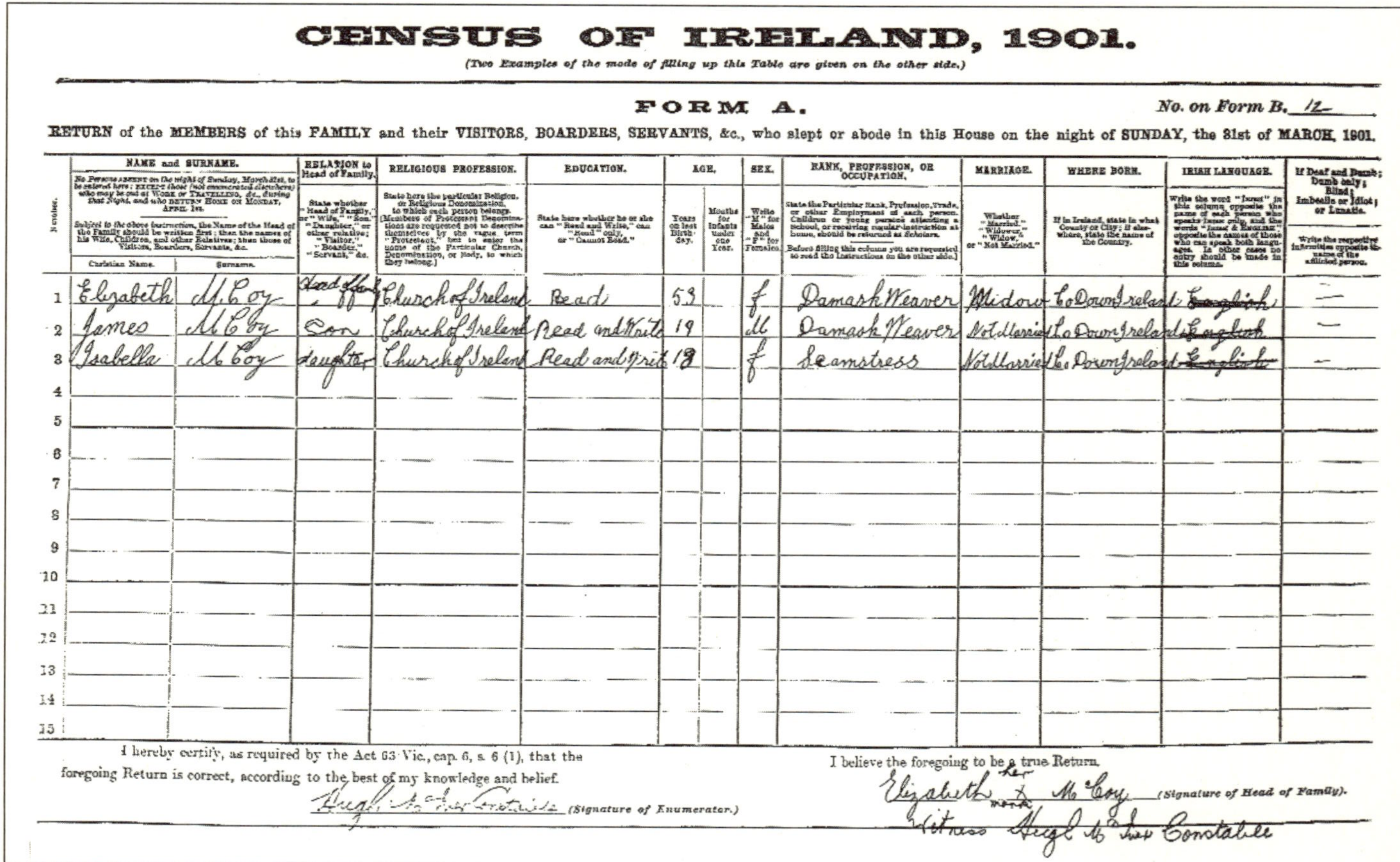

CENSUS OF IRELAND, 1901.

(Two Examples of the mode of filling up this Table are given on the other side.)

FORM A.

No. on Form B. 12

RETURN of the MEMBERS of this FAMILY and their VISITORS, BOARDERS, SERVANTS, &c., who slept or abode in this House on the night of SUNDAY, the 31st of MARCH, 1901.

Number	Christian Name	Surname	Relation to Head of Family	Religious Profession	Education	Age: Years on last Birthday	Age: Months for Infants under one Year	Sex	Rank, Profession, or Occupation	Marriage	Where Born	Irish Language	If Deaf and Dumb; Dumb only; Blind; Imbecile or Idiot; or Lunatic
1	Elizabeth	McCoy	Head of Family	Church of Ireland	Read	53		F	Damask Weaver	Widow	Co Down Ireland	~~English~~	–
2	James	McCoy	Son	Church of Ireland	Read and Write	19		M	Damask Weaver	Not Married	Co Down Ireland	~~English~~	–
3	Isabella	McCoy	Daughter	Church of Ireland	Read and Write	18		F	Seamstress	Not Married	Co Down Ireland	~~English~~	–
4													
5													
6													
7													
8													
9													
10													
11													
12													
13													
14													
15													

I hereby certify, as required by the Act 63 Vic., cap. 6, s. 6 (1), that the foregoing Return is correct, according to the best of my knowledge and belief.

Hugh McIvor Constable (Signature of Enumerator.)

I believe the foregoing to be a true Return.

Elizabeth her x mark McCoy (Signature of Head of Family).

Witness Hugh McIvor Constable

Household Return of McCoy family. 1901 Census, County Down. DED 91/19, Moira, Gortnamoney townland. Reproduced by kind permission of the National Archives.

cambric handloom weaving and sewing. He suggests that the continued availability of linen weaving and sewing helped control the immediate post-Famine emigration which was common throughout Ireland and that it was only in the 1880s and 1890s, when powered linen manufacture successfully competed with handloom production, that this district began to see a decline in its population. In 1901, linen workers still predominated, occupying three out of every four houses and averaging more than two to a house. Both women and men were handloom weavers and 13 per cent of them were over retirement age. The ageing of the community was a portent of the demise of domestic handloom weaving.

The 1901 census schedules of a town can also provide a straightforward means of understanding the social profile of an urban community in the early twentieth century. Cohen's work on Gilford, the linen factory town in Tullylish parish near Portadown, County Armagh, and less than ten miles from Moira, uncovered the extent to which the employment in the linen mill and factories influenced the living patterns of the families revealed in the census schedules.[8] Two aspects of these patterns, status and gender, have a significance far beyond the study of the individual community. The status differences in earnings based on skilled and unskilled work separated Protestant and Catholic families for there were twice as many Protestant mechanics as Catholics and three times as many Protestant artisans and craftsmen. Skilled workers' wages were sufficient to maintain their families but unskilled labourers' families could generally only 'make ends meet' when either their wives or their children were at work. As proportionately more Catholic men were in unskilled work, more of their wives and daughters were employed in the linen mill. The dominance of the linen industry, with its emphasis on the employment of women and young people, also meant that Tullylish was a place where women and young people could gain a living. Almost one third of the households in Tullylish were headed by women, 60 per cent of whom were listed as widows. Although many of the widows worked, their principal support was in the earnings of their children, especially their adult daughters, working in the Gilford linen mill of Dunbar McMaster & Co. There was a clear diversity between the upbringing in a Protestant skilled worker's household with a regular wage and a Catholic widow's household where the livelihood was earned by young people who had left school early to earn money in the mill.

A further use of the 1901 census material can be in the study of a social grouping such as a social class or occupation. Maguire's study of the Dublin Protestant working class used selected 1901 schedules for three neighbourhoods in Dublin: Wexford Street-Aungier Street, where the only significant employer was Jacob's biscuit factory; South Circular Road, a mixed district of older two-roomed dwellings off Clanbrassil Street and newly built 5-8 bedroomed terraced houses on South Circular Road itself; the working class suburb of Inchicore which was built around the yards and workshops of the Great Southern and Western Railway and the Dublin United Tramway Company.[9] In contrast to Belfast at the same period, examined by Hepburn and Collins, there was no marked religious residential clustering in Dublin.[10] Social class determined where people lived and what type of houses they lived in. Linking the census to marriage registers, Maguire found that, among the working class, religiously mixed marriages were relatively common (generally between Protestant men and Catholic women). Most of the offspring were baptized and reared as Catholics, not following a perceived tradition of sons following their fathers' religion and daughters following that of their mothers. The 1907 papal Ne Temere decree merely reinforced an already prevalent pattern. The outcome of these individual actions, plus the marked mobility of young single men, which was apparent between the censuses, set in motion a decline in the Protestant working class in Dublin, even before the disruptive effects of the War of Independence and the Civil War upon industrial life in Dublin.

Throughout the British Isles, the most common occupation for women before the First World War was domestic service and Mona Hearn's study demonstrates the value of using the census schedules (of the 1911 census) in conjunction with a wide range of other source material, including oral history, biographies, family papers and government publications.[11] Servant-keeping varied according to social class; while 23 per cent of the Dublin lower middle class had at least one servant, 71 per cent of the middle class and 98 per cent of the upper class had servants. Comparatively few worked in 'big houses' with large domestic staff. Most servants were young single women working in houses where only one servant was employed. They were responsible, along with the housewife, for the smooth running of the household. At number 54, Grosvenor Square, Rathmines in 1911, lived Ellen Quillan, a twenty-five year old single Catholic servant girl from County Fermanagh, in the household of Robert Daly, a civil servant in the telegraph department of the GPO, which included his wife and three teenage children. Number 54 had twelve granite steps leading up to the front door, cleaned by Ellen. Kitchen premises were in the basement below. Ellen had to carry all meals from the basement up to the first floor dining room, light the ranges and fires, carry hot water up to the bedrooms and dirty water down again, clean the house, and cook and serve meals.

In country areas, servant work was heavy and the routine relentless when it included looking after fowl, cows and pigs. Hearn used oral history to tease out the nuances. A girl's first 'situation' was often a prelude to a lifetime in service; 'one former servant who left school at 11 years of age...was treated as one of the family, called the farmer and his wife 'Daddy and Mammy' but got no pay. She then went to another farm…where she had board and lodging and 'they dressed her' but she had no regular wage. It was only after these experiences that she got a 'proper job' as a scullery maid in a big house in County Meath'.[12] A scullery maid's duties confined her to the kitchen quarters, preparing vegetables and washing the used saucepans and cooking pots, and dishes from the dining room. She was under the direction of the cook and, if satisfactory, might have progressed to the position of kitchen maid.

The possession and entitlement to land, a key feature of Irish life at a national as well as a local level, can also be examined through linking land valuation records to the censuses. Breen's use of the land valuation records of the late nineteenth and early twentieth century and the 1911 census enumeration schedules for a district in County Kerry enabled him to identify the relationship between family structure and landholding patterns.[13] Individual families were traced in the land valuation material and linked to the population documented in the census. Breen was able to demonstrate how family relationships and the economic and social standing of those who had disappeared or 'moved away' could be linked, first, to changes in local social structure arising from the Irish Famine of the 1840s and second, to the change to pastoral farming with its diminished need for farm labour. Those who disappeared from the land valuation records in the later nineteenth century were from the families of farm labourers (those with no permanent entitlement to land) and the non-inheriting grown up children of farmers. The outcome of this self-selected out-movement was visible in the lack of diversity in farm holdings in 1911. The census schedules showed that the strong family farm had become the typical homestead in the community with few rural tradesmen or professionals. This trend was counter to that prevailing in most of western Europe at the time, when other rural communities were being depleted by the permanent emigration of entire families. Moreover, various legislative policies in the late nineteenth and early twentieth century served to strengthen the local power base of 'strong farmers'; these included the broadening of the franchise in the 1880s, the establishment of representative district councils in 1898 and the land legislation providing for owner occupation during the period leading up to 1914.

Study of the early twentieth-century census schedules in Ireland provides, above all, a privileged entry into the lives of a past generation. The abundance of social history is waiting there for the reader to interpret. Of course there are issues of judgment to be made: over legibility; over apparent inconsistencies in relationships (where, for example, a step child could be enumerated as an in-law); and apparent inconsistencies in ages (due to the tendency to 'round up', especially in the 1911 census after the old age pension, payable at 5 shillings-weekly, had been introduced in 1908 for those aged 70 and above). Wives' occupations, too, are generally thought to have been under-recorded. Nevertheless, as a primary source for the study of the social history of early twentieth century Ireland, the census schedules have an authenticity, a provenance, and an immediacy which is hard to surpass. Turning over the pages or, to a lesser degree, winding through a microfilm reel, of streets upon city streets of mill workers and their families, or of a townland, already depleted in 1901, but where the family surnames still persist to this day, enables that 'double sense of great closeness and great distance'[14] within which to interpret both the past and the present.

NOTES

1 Stephen A. Royle, 'Irish Manuscript Census Records: A Neglected Source of Information' *Irish Geography*, Vol. II, 1978, pp 110-125.

2 B. Collins, 'The Analysis of Census Returns: the 1901 Census of Ireland', *Ulster Local Studies*, vol.15, no.1, 1993, pp. 38-46; P. Collins, *Pathways to Ulster's Past* (Belfast, 1998).

3 W.A. Maguire, *A Century in Focus* (Belfast, 2000), p. 154.

4 William H. Crawford, 'Creating the Framework', in W.H. Crawford & R.H. Foy, *Townlands in Ulster* (Belfast, 1998), p. 22.

5 Graham Mawhinney, 'Owenreagh, County Londonderry', in W.H. Crawford & R.H. Foy, *Townlands in Ulster* (Belfast, 1998), pp. 230-1.

6 B. Collins, 'The Loom, the Land and the Marketplace: Women Weavers and the Family Economy in Late Nineteenth and Early Twentieth Century Ireland', in Marilyn Cohen, *The Warp of Ulster's Past. Interdisciplinary Perspectives on the Irish Linen Industry 1700-1920*, (Manchester, 1997), pp. 229-252.

7 W.H. Crawford, 'A Handloom Weaving Community in County Down' *Ulster Folklife*, 39 (1993), pp. 1-14.

8 Marilyn Cohen, *Linen, Family and Community in Tullylish, County Down 1690-1914* (Dublin, 1997).

9 Martin Maguire, 'A Socio-Economic Analysis of the Dublin Protestant Working Class 1870-1926', *Irish Economic and Social History*, XX, 1993, pp. 35-61.

10 A.C. Hepburn and B. Collins, 'Industrial Society: the Structure of Belfast, 1901', in P. Roebuck, *Plantation to Partition. Essays in Honour of J.L. McCracken* (Belfast, 1981), pp. 210-228.

11 Mona Hearn, *Below Stairs* (Dublin, 1993).

12 Hearn, pp. 2-3.

13 R. Breen, 'Population Trends in Late Nineteenth and early Twentieth Century Ireland; a local study' *Economic and Social Review*, 15, 2, (1984), pp. 95-108.

14 Seamus Heaney, 'The Sense of the Past', *History Ireland*, Vol.1, no. 4, (1993), p. 37.

1901 CENSUS ENUMERATORS' RETURNS ONLINE

Margaret Brennand

From 2 January 2002 researchers will be able to have access to the 1901 Census returns for England and Wales, held at the Public Record Office in Kew. This date is eagerly awaited by family historians world-wide. Unlike the census returns for Ireland which have been available for public consultation in the National Archives, Dublin, for some years, those for England and Wales are subject to a hundred year closure. The census returns are undoubtedly the Public Record Office's most popular historical records; being a key source for those researching family trees, local areas or the history of a house. They also provide much of the raw data for local, social and economic historians.

For the first time these key records will be available over the Internet at www.census.pro.gov.uk.

The vision at the Public Record Office is to make our services and records available electronically on-site and remotely via the Internet. The result will be widely available services not only in the United Kingdom and Ireland but also world-wide. A key project for achieving our vision has been the digitisation of the 1901 Census returns for England and Wales.

Why are we doing this? If you want to look at census returns for the nineteenth century you currently have two options. The first is to visit your local record office or library which usually house the returns for the locality. The second option is to travel to the Family Records Centre in London which houses the census returns for England and Wales from 1841 to 1891.

However, many users find it expensive to travel to the south-east and many are simply unable to get to our reading rooms because of domestic or work commitments. We also feel that, as we are the National Archive for England and Wales, we have a duty to serve all citizens and we should make our services more widely available. We see the Internet as an ideal medium to meet the needs of our ever-growing group of users, and more and more researchers are using the Internet to access information to further their research.

The 1901 Census

The 1901 Census for England and Wales was taken on 31 March 1901. The population at the time was over 32 million and these 32 million entries will be available online for the very first time from the first working day of January 2002. Never before will it have been so easy to learn of those who lived in Edwardian times; to understand their work; to trace the homes they lived in and to speculate on the lives they led.

Information on the Census return

The following information can be found in the nineteenth-century census returns:

* Road, street, number or name of house
* Whether the house is inhabited or not
* Name and surname of each person
* Relation to Head of Family
* Condition as to marriage
* Age last birthday
* Profession or occupation
* Whether employed or not
* Where born
* Whether deaf and dumb, blind, lunatic, imbecile or feeble-minded

The 1901 Census returns are in very much a similar format and have just minor additions.

(a) The inhabited/uninhabited column asks if the house is in occupation or is being built.
(b) The employment details have been expanded and ask if working at home.
(c) Returns for Wales and the Isle of Man have an extra column for the language spoken.

1901 Census Online: how are we achieving this? Putting the 1901 Census returns online involves many people working busily behind the scenes on the three elements of the digitisation project. Firstly we have had to create electronic images of the census returns themselves. The images have been scanned from the archival microfilm copy of the returns and a high quality digitised image produced. Secondly, we have created a database of information transcribed from the census returns. This will allow us to provide users with a means of accessing and navigating the data more flexibly and readily than by traditional means. Users will be able to conduct a number of searches and, having found an individual, go directly to the images of the returns. Thirdly the database will be linked to the digital images and the whole service put on the Internet.

Using the 1901 Online Census

To provide the most cost-effective method of utilising these census returns we have endeavoured to ensure that all basic searches are free and you will be able to conduct a number of different types of searches; for example by name, place, address, institution or vessel.

Person search

We expect that many inquirers will wish to search by name and a typical name search in the 1901 online service will work as follows: you can undertake a basic search using name (forenames and surnames), place and age. If a surname is double-barrelled you will need to search on each element. For example, for someone with the surname 'Lloyd-Gibson' you would search on 'Lloyd' and 'Gibson' and if you are unsure of the age of the person you wish to locate you will be able to input a range of years. A feature of this basic search will be:

* Wildcards for single or multiple characters. For example 'BR*N' which would enable you to locate all those names beginning with BR and ending in N with any combination of letters in between. Results of this search would include names such as Brown, Braun and Broughton.

If you find that your basic search results in too many returns, then you can undertake an advanced search which enables you to use a variety of other search fields with which to refine your search strategy. This is particularly useful if you are searching for a popular surname which may result in a large number of returns. Features on the advance search will include:

* Soundex match which enables you to identify names with similar phonetics, for example 'Brown' and 'Browne'.
* Synonyms and abbreviations; that is where if you provide a full forename the system will return matching synonyms and abbreviations. For example, a search for John will also return references to Jon, Jack and Jno.

You will also be able to search on forename only (an important facility for those looking for female ancestors without knowing their maiden name).

Once you have completed your search and found the individual you require, you have two options:

* Firstly you can view a digital image of the census return. The image will be a complete page from the original enumeration book which will typically include more than one household and all the residents within. This image will cost 75p. Once you have bought the image you can save it to your own system and/or print out a copy. If you do not have printing facilities at home you will be able to place an order online and a copy will be posted to you.
* Secondly you can view transcribed details from the census returns relating to an individual. This will cost 50p. If you wish to view the details of all those resident in the same household you can do this for an extra 50p.

Other searches

We realise that researchers will wish to use the census returns for other types of information (eg relating to a place). You will be able to do a basic search by place and a more advanced search by place using the features described above. If you know the address for your household you can simply type it in. If your ancestor was on a vessel or in an institution (eg workhouse) then you can do special searches which will identify the vessel or institution and detail all those on board or dwelling there on Census Night.

Help and guidance

We will have sample searches so that you can try out the system to see how it works. There will also be comprehensive sets of technical help and search tips for getting the best out of the system. We are also preparing a booklet for those users who would prefer to read about the service before going online.

Methods of payment

We expect that most of you will wish to purchase your digital images or transcripts by credit card and we are able to accept Visa, MasterCard, American Express and Debit Cards (Switch/Delta). Unfortunately we will not be able to accept Diners Club cards.

If you do not wish to use a credit card you will be able to buy vouchers to use the 1901 Census service (in units of £5, £10 and £50). We expect these vouchers to be on sale at record offices and libraries throughout the UK and a list of those places selling vouchers will be published on the website. Full details of the ways to pay will be on the census website.

Where to access the online service

More and more people are being connected to the Internet and so can view the 1901 returns from the comfort of their own homes. People without Internet access can go to their local library, record office or Cyber Café; in fact anywhere that provides Internet access.

Users have a choice

There will be some users who still prefer to look at the census returns on more traditional formats. We recognize this and will provide free access to a set of the 1901 returns on microfiche along with the standard finding aids in our reading rooms at Kew. In addition, many local record offices and libraries have bought microform copies of the 1901 returns for their own areas.

However we do feel that once you have tried the online service you will find it a much more cost effective service than travelling to Kew. A database of over 32 million names searchable for free is only available as part of the online service.

Exciting new plans

Throughout the 1901 Census Online Project we were asked about our plans for digitising the earlier censuses and making them available over the Internet. The 1901 Census Project has paved the way for digitising the earlier censuses and we have decided to go forward with the 1881 and 1891 censuses even before the 1901 was released.

Our aim is to have both the 1881 and 1891 censuses available over the Internet by the end of 2002.

1891 Census Online

Work began on scanning the 1891 returns in the summer of 2001 and the first county (London) should be available in the spring of 2002. Other counties will soon follow (probably those with large cities as a first priority). Initially users will be able to access the 1891 returns through a basic name index. Once all the counties are complete the index will be enhanced with more searchable fields.

1881 Census Online

Work began on scanning the 1881 returns in the summer of 2001 and these will be linked to the GSU (Genealogical Society of Utah) database. The aim is to have the full 1881 index, transcription and original images all available over the Internet by the end of 2002.

A wonderful resource for the future

The Public Record Office is pleased at the progress of Census Online and we feel we are now offering a significant service to family historians and many other researchers. Census Online is still only part of our programme (called The Nation's Memory) to make available many other record series and services over the Internet.

Censuses for Ireland and Scotland

The General Register Office for Scotland is also planning to put the 1901 Census returns for Scotland on the Internet. For more information visit their website at http://wood.ccta.gov.uk/grosweb/grosweb.nsf/pages/home We are not aware of any immediate digitisation plans for the Irish censuses but once the 1901 service goes online we are sure that our colleagues in Ireland will be considering this.

Consultation and communication

We have kept in regular contact with those interested in our work throughout the 1901 Census Online project and will continue to do so as the next censuses are underway. If you have access to the Internet you can visit our census web site at <www.census.pro.gov.uk> for regular updates on Census.

Online

We have also established a special panel to advise us on the development of Census Online. The following organisations are represented:

Federation of Family History Societies
Society of Genealogists
Guild of One-Name Studies
Association of Genealogists and Record Agents
British Association for Local History
University of Essex
Minutes of the meetings of this Advisory Panel are posted on the website and displayed on the 1901 notice board at the FRC.

Events in 2002

Members of the 1901 Team will be attending a range of events in 2002 to promote Census Online. This will include some of the larger genealogical fairs (eg London, York, Liverpool) and we hope to be at a venue in Wales in the autumn. Keep an eye on the website for up-to-date details.

Regular information

Regular information is available on the census web site <www.census.pro.gov.uk>. If you wish to speak to someone about Census Online please telephone: 020 8392 5200.

JAMES FULLTON: A PHILADELPHIA MERCHANT AND HIS CUSTOMERS

Richard K. McMaster

By the middle years of the eighteenth century business firms in Londonderry, Belfast, and Newry had established commercial links with Philadelphia, New York, and other American ports. Their agents shipped cargoes of flaxseed, flour, wheat, iron, timber, and barrel staves to Ulster ports. Since flaxseed had to arrive in ample time for spring planting, there was a seasonal rhythm to the trade. On the arrival of the flaxseed ships their owners advertised for passengers, redemptioners (whose fares were paid on arrival, usually by family members) and indentured servants for the outward passage to America. These ships would also carry an assortment of Irish linens, beef, potatoes, gammons and other items to sell in the Colonies. If the emigrant ships arrived early in the season, there would be time for an additional voyage to one of the Southern or West Indian colonies before taking on flaxseed and flour in Philadelphia to sail for home in November or December. Early arrival at Derry or Belfast permitted flaxseed ships to fit in another voyage to Bristol or Norway before embarking passengers for the Colonies. Every firm trading to America needed a trusted and competent man on the spot to handle each stage of a complicated business transaction.

One such man was James Fullton, a Philadelphia merchant with connections in Londonderry and Rathmelton, Co. Donegal. Descendants of James Fullton found a collection of ledgers and a letter book in the attic of his retirement home in York County, Pennsylvania, in 1938 and saw to their preservation. They are now available to researchers in the Library of the Historical Society of York County, 250 East Market Street, York, Pennsylvania.

James Fullton and his clerks spelled his surname Fullton, as did a kinsman of the same name whose Lancaster County, Pennsylvania home is now in the Ulster-American Folk Park, Omagh, Co. Tyrone. The merchant's brother John and all of their American descendants have used the spelling Fulton. He had a brother in Rathmelton, Co. Donegal, and cousins in Londonderry, but the date and place of James Fullton's birth and the year of his emigration are not known.

Family connections were important for James Fullton. Both his Ulster correspondents and his American customers included kinfolk. Fullton addressed Derry merchant James Martin as 'Dear Brother,' suggesting Martin had married Fullton's sister, and called James Fullton, Jr., another Londonderry merchant, his 'kinsman.' Writing to his brother John Fullton in Rathmelton in 1766, he noted the safe arrival in Philadelphia of their brother Thomas and his family.[1] John Fullton also came to America with his family in 1773. Fullton also shipped flour and iron to his 'kinsman' Andrew Black in Boston. His Pennsylvania associates included other family members. Moses Black of Chestnut Level, Drumore Township, Lancaster County, who supplied Fullton with flour was Andrew Black's brother. Still another kinsman was James Fullton of Donegal Township, Lancaster County, who had many dealings with the Pennsylvania merchant. Robert Fulton of Lancaster was another customer and possibly a family member, too. He was the father of the well-known artist and steamboat builder of the same name.

On 28 February 1760 James Fullton was married to Mary Moore, daughter of Walter Moore of Moreland, Philadelphia (now Montgomery) County, Pennsylvania. The Rev. John Cuthbertson married the couple. He was a Covenanter, the first missionary of the Reformed Presbyterian Church in North America and the husband of Mary Moore's sister Sally.[2]

In 1763 James Fullton and his father-in-law advertised for sale a farm of 180 acres, two-thirds cleared, in the Manor of Moreland and a grist mill on Pennypack Creek, 'formerly occupied by Walter Moore.'[3] Walter Moore had moved in with his daughter and son-in-law before that, since Fullton charged Moore's estate 'For his boarding, washing and lodging and his lukens found him at my house from 1 January 1762 to 15 May 1766 being 4 yr. 4 mo. at £40 per annum. £174.16.0.'[4]

He was in business in Philadelphia in 1758 in partnership with Valentine Standley. Like most merchants of their time and place, they operated a general store. They advertised a variety of goods for sale at their store on the north side of Market Street, a little below Water Street, including 'A good Assortment of yd., yd. 7/8ths, and 3 qr. Checks, Shalloons, striped Linens, Fustians, Camblets and Delf-ware opened, choice Antigua Rum, Philadelphia ditto, Muscavado Sugar, Loaf ditto, Tea, Coffee, also a likely young Negroe Boy, that has had the Small

Pox.'[5] In later advertisements they offered 'Choice Madeira and Lisbon Wines, West India and Philadelphia Rum, Muscavado and White Sugars, Cocoa, Coffee, Tea, Chocolate, Pepper, Allspice, best French Indigo, Rice, Mackerel, Oil, &c.'[6] The firm owned a share of the ship *Mohawk* with Andrew Hodge and Co. for trading voyages to the West Indies and Quebec (Ledger A.). Fullton and Standley dissolved their partnership in October 1760.[7]

James Fullton was now in business on his own. He retained their store on Market Street, but narrowed the range of products he sold there to 'Jamaica Spirit, West India and Philadelphia Rum, Muscavado and Loaf Sugar, Madeira and sundry other Wines, Tea, Coffee, Pepper, Pimento, &c.'[8] In Fullton's ledgers they are the only items listed in his 'Merchandize Account.' Fullton kept them in stock at all times. He sold and advertised other items from time to time, notably Irish linens, beef and gammons, but these were shipped to him on consignment by his overseas correspondents and credited to their accounts.

Fullton shipped rum, wine, sugar, and tea in wholesale quantities by wagon to customers who kept taverns and general stores along the arc of Scotch-Irish settlement in Pennsylvania from Chester and Lancaster counties to Harris' Ferry (Harrisburg), Carlisle, Shippensburg, Chambersburg and Marsh Creek (Gettysburg). On occasion Fullton sent madeira and rum by wagon over the mountains to Fort Ligonier in western Pennsylvania. He also supplied customers in Maryland and Delaware, sending the goods by boat. Although he sold goods in common use among Colonists of every ethnic background, Fullton's customers and suppliers were nearly all of Ulster birth or parentage.

His clerks generally identified customers by their residence when making up the day books and ledgers. In many cases they are identified by the Presbyterian congregation in their neighborhood. Some are given detailed locations, as Elijah Sinclair 'over Susquehanna River near Nelsons Ferry York County.' A partial list of Pennsylvanians would include Thomas Orr 'Bucks County,' William Thompson 'Brandywine,' Revd John Cuthbertson, Humphrey Fullerton and Joseph Walker 'Octororo' in Chester County, John Elliott, John Houston, John Parkes and Samuel Scott 'Pequea', Moses Black, Andrew Boyd, Joseph Larimore and William Steel 'Chestnut Level,' William Allison, Joseph Boyd, Robert Fulton, John Long, William Montgomery and John Shaw 'Lancaster,' John Bayly, Margaret Craig, James Fullton, Stewart Rowan and Col. Patrick Work 'Donegal,' all in present Lancaster County, Thomas Black 'Swatara,' William McCullough 'Paxton' and John Orr, Samuel Simpson and James Wood 'at Harris' Ferry' all in present Dauphin County, John Agnew, Capt. Robert Callendar, John Fullton, Robert Hanna, Robert Miller, John Montgomery, Esq., James Parker, James Pollock, Joseph Spear and John Trindle 'Carlisle' and Cleary Campbell, Robert Cuthbertson, John Elliott, David Magaw, James McCall and Samuel Montgomery 'Shippensburg' in present Cumberland County, Col. Benjamin Chambers 'Rocky Spring' (Chambersburg) and John Clark, William McCrea, and James Robeson 'Conococheague' in present Franklin County, Samuel Gettys and Joseph Morrison 'Marsh Creek' in present Adams County, George Erwin and John Moore 'York Town' and Sampson Archer, David Hunter and John McKinly 'York County.'

He also dealt with William Spear and (John) Smith and (James) Sterrett in 'Baltimore Town' and (Thomas) Harris and (William) McClure in present Harford County, Maryland, with Robert Martin at Chestertown on Maryland's Eastern Shore and with Allan Gillespie at Newark and George Thompson at Christiana Bridge in Delaware. In addition, Fullton regularly did business with Charles Crawford and Samuel Smyth in Newbern, North Carolina, and with Andrew Black and Hugh Orr in Boston.

Philadelphia was the nodal point for shipping American grain, especially flour, to the West Indies, southern Europe, New England, and even the British Isles. The flaxseed trade, exclusively with Irish ports, rose to major proportions after 1740. Pennsylvania iron became an important export by 1750. Philadelphia merchants scoured the province and neighbouring parts of Maryland and Delaware for these commodities, often through local agents.[9]

Besides selling goods at retail and wholesale, James Fullton bought flour and flaxseed to send to his business associates in Ulster. Assembling cargoes and loading ships to their orders was a major part of his operation in the flaxseed season. He purchased flour from millers in south-eastern Pennsylvania, such as Moses Black, John Boyd, James Cochran, John Graves, Joseph Hart, Charles Hay, Henry Hoover, Robert Jones, Joseph Paul and John Thompson, and had it inspected and graded in Philadelphia, dispatching it to Londonderry at different times in the year. In contrast, the flaxseed season was short and rushed. Fullton advanced cash to flaxseed buyers to help him fill orders from Londonderry merchants. Fullton had Hugh McCullough clean and grade all his flaxseed in November with little time left before the ships sailed for Derry and other Ulster ports. His flaxseed suppliers included James Baird, John Calbreath, Daniel Clark, Seth Duncan, George Erwin, Samuel Gettys, John Jones, Hugh King, Robert Lindsay, Charles Linn, Robert Martin, Alexander Miller, Joseph Miller, Thomas Montgomery, Hugh Ross, Elijah Sinclair, Robert Thompson, and Robert White, supplemented by purchases from the Philadelphia mercantile firms of William and Andrew Caldwell, Barnet Gratz, Levi Hollingsworth and Samuel Purviance, Sr. to fill out a cargo in time.[10]

Fullton made periodic tours around the circuit of his customers in Pennsylvania, Delaware and Maryland later having his clerk record 'Sundry Accounts received at their houses' in his Day Book. The receipts are in no particular order so it is impossible to reconstruct his route. He probably purchased flour and other goods on these trips.

At one time Fullton was associated with James Harvey, a Londonderry merchant temporarily in Philadelphia. In November 1762 James Harvey advertised for passengers and cargo for the ship *Rose*, Captain William Hope, about to sail for Londonderry. A year later Fullton advertised the same ship and captain for Londonderry.[11] On her 1763 voyage the *Rose* carried 200 hogsheads of flaxseed addressed to James Harvey and Co., 42 hogsheads consigned to James Martin of Londonderry, 40 hogsheads for James Chambers of Londonderry, and 25 hogsheads each for Fullton's brother John in Rathmelton, Co. Donegal and Richard Floyd 'near Rathmelton.'[12] The *Rose* of Londonderry made many crossings with flaxseed and flour for Ireland and emigrants, linen, and other cargo for Pennsylvania. James Harvey was one of her owners.[13] His stay in America was brief and he was Burgess of Londonderry at the time of his death in 1772.[14]

In December 1764 James Fullton dispatched the *Rose*, Captain Joseph McNutt, for Londonderry with a cargo of flaxseed consigned to James Harvey and Co. Fullton also shipped flour and flaxseed to James Gamble of Londonderry on this voyage. He instructed Captain McNutt to take on passengers and sail for Philadelphia on the return voyage by 15 April or 1 May at the latest. The *Rose* was a week late in departing Philadelphia and was caught in the ice on the Delaware.[15]

The flaxseed trade was steady, with supply and demand predictable from year to year.[16] But market share was not constant and agents had to shift emphasis from flaxseed to flour and wheat and back. A year later, for instance, in December 1765, Fullton shipped Harvey and Company by the *Rose* 339 barrels of flour, 55 hogsheads of flaxseed, 1,872 bushels of wheat, 86 barrels of ship bread and 1,795 barrel staves.[17]

Besides the six merchants already mentioned, Fullton's ledgers and letters indicate that he shipped flaxseed and flour to other Derry merchants and handled sales of linen and other products for them. He regularly sold linens for James Martin, James Fullton, Jr., John King, John Fullton and Richard Floyd. Samuel Currey shipped him beef, butter and potatoes from Derry, as did James Harvey. He filled flaxseed commissions for Dickson Cunningham, Robert Edmiston, James Gamble, John and William Henry, William Linn, Archibald Montgomery, William Thompson and other Londonderry merchants.

By 1764 Fullton was part owner of another ship in the flaxseed and emigrant trade. The *Hibernia*, a ship of 193 tons, was built for Fullton at Simon Sherlock's yard on the Delaware. Sherlock received payment for the hull in April 1764. The ledgers include a long list of ship chandler, boat builder, sail makers, block maker, painter, mast maker, blacksmith, joiner, rigger, and other artisans whose final accounts were settled in January 1765, including Brian Wilkinson who carved a lion's head for the ship's bow. The ledgers also have accounts for provisioning the ship, rum 'furnished sundry passengers in order to engage their passage,' wages and provisions for the mate and sailors, and 'drink for her launch.'

The *Hibernia* was ready for sea in November 1764, when Fullton announced:

> For Londonderry, the Ship *Hibernia*, William Keith, Master, Will sail about the Twenty fifth of this last November, having great Part of her Cargo now on board, has good Accommodations for Passengers. For Freight or Passage, apply to James Fullton.[18]

The *Hibernia*'s owners were James Fullton of Philadelphia, his brother John Fullton of Rathmelton, Co. Donegal, and Ephraim Campbell of Londonderry. She returned to Philadelphia with emigrants in 1765 and again in 1766. Campbell and Fullton and Ninian Boggs announced the *Hibernia* would sail from Londonderry for Newcastle, Delaware, and Philadelphia on 1 August 1765.[19] They again advertised in the *Belfast News Letter* in February 1766 for passengers, redemptioners and servants for *Hibernia*'s return voyage from Londonderry to Newcastle and Philadelphia. James Fullton reported their safe arrival in May 1766.[20]

As soon as the emigrants landed, Fullton normally sent his ship from Philadelphia with a cargo of pig iron and bar iron consigned to Henry Cruger of Bristol. The iron came from Martick Furnace in Lancaster County, Pennsylvania, which Fullton owned in partnership with two associates. He gave instructions to Captain William Keith to sail the *Hibernia* for Philadelphia by 20 August 'and return here for a flaxseed freight.' She would carry flaxseed to Londonderry and come back to Philadelphia with emigrants.[21]

Ships had to adhere to a tight schedule like this in order to turn a profit for their owners. Fullton complained that 'to ly at Derry for Passengers till the middle of Summer and make Only one Voyage in the year will not in my opinion by any means Do.' It was essential to send 'the Ship from Derry for this Port by the middle of April at farthest.'[22]

Fullton had the *Hibernia* loaded with flaxseed and ready to sail in December 1766, but only with difficulty. An early frost blocked rivers and creeks and kept flaxseed from reaching Philadelphia by shallop. A short supply raised prices.[23]

John Fullton of Rathmelton, Ephraim Campbell and Ninian Boggs of Londonderry were agents for the *Hibernia* in 1767.[24] They dispatched her to Norway before she sailed for Philadelphia with passengers, so the ship again came late in the season. James Fullton was unhappy with their decision, as 'it would put the Ship out of the way of a flaxseed freight home in the fall.' Captain Keith sailed with the flaxseed ships in November 1767, but with a cargo of timber and Martic Furnace iron for Bristol.[25]

Word eventually reached Philadelphia of the loss of the *Hibernia* in Bristol Channel. The first news was good. All on board were safe and ship and cargo insured. James Fullton nevertheless suffered serious financial reverses:

> Which Loses might have been Remedead to us if that onnerthey ongreatfull Ignorant Fellow Keith had purchased the wrake of the Ship for our acc[oun]t when sold at such a Triffle as £100 – by which we should have saved at Least 4 or 500£ Sterling as the hull would have Sold for 2 or 300 and the materrells would have been worth I am sure £400 Sterling to us. Besides on his sending the materrells to me I could Easily and on Low terms have purchased the Hull of a Ship here and so Continued a Vessall in the tread.[26]

Fullton never again had a vessel in the trade. He had continued to act as James Harvey's agent in finding cargoes for the *Rose* and other vessels, but in 1767 Fullton received a letter from James Harvey 'Giving your Reasons for addressing your Ship to another house' and terminating their business arrangement.[27]

James Fullton found it necessary to press his brother John Fullton for payment of outstanding bills, 'as I have Suffered so Havely in Supporting him both in Creditt and Interest, it would add to my mortification to Loan the balance now Dew me by him.'[28]

Fullton's investment in iron manufacturing turned sour at the same time. In 1761 William Smith and William Bennett, Lancaster County ironmasters, and Samuel Webb, an ironmaster in Maryland, leased a two-thirds interest in Martick Forge and Furnace in Lancaster County, Pennsylvania, to James Fulton and James Wallace, merchants of Philadelphia. In 1764 they sold it to Fullton and Wallace as tenants in common. James Wallace had been in business as a general merchant as early as 1748 and formed a partnership with George Bryan in 1752; he continued in business with Thomas Wallace as partner after 1755.[29] The remaining one third interest belonged to Thomas Smith who operated the ironworks.

The three partners advertised Martick Forge and Furnace for sale in the *Pennsylvania Gazette* in 1767, providing a brief description of the ironworks.

> To be sold, Martick Furnace, with the Forge, and about 4,000 acres of land thereunto belonging, remarkably well-wooded, situated on a branch of Pequea, in Lancaster County, province of Pennsylvania, the furnace, casting-bellows, and bridge houses are built of stone, completely and substantially finished; a large coal house; several convenient houses for the workmen, &c. good pasture fields, well fenced, a great deal of meadow, and more easily may be made, having never failing springs. There is a large quantity of coal and ore at the furnace, a considerable quantity of wood ready cut in the woods, for coaling; a very good bank of ore three miles distant from the works; the water never fails, nor can they receive the least injury from the greatest floods; a good grist mill, two stories high, of stone, and the lands adjacent well timbered; the forge is situated on Pequea, four miles from the furnace, has four fires, two hammers, two coal-houses, and other necessary buildings, in good order; the whole stock, white servants, negroes, horses, waggons &c. will be sold also. The purchaser paying a fourth of the purchase money down, may have time given for the remainder. For terms, apply to Thomas Smith, living near the works, or to James Wallace, and James Fullton, in Philadelphia.[30]

They apparently found no purchaser. Strapped for cash after the loss of the *Hibernia*, Fullton asked his London correspondent David Harvey to arrange a mortgage on his own third of the Martick complex. 'I purchased it in november 1765, for ye third part I gave £3,350.0.0 [Pennsylvania] Currency and it was thought a Good Purchase by the best judges.' If Harvey could not find someone willing to loan money on this security, Fullton asked him to 'apply to some Gentelman that Shipes goods to America for £1,500 worth of store goods on long credit.'

In May 1768 Fullton had mortgaged his share in the Martick works to James Wallace to secure payment of £3,500 that he owed Wallace. This mortgage was secured by 1,570 acres belonging to Martick Forge and mine bank, furniture at the Forge and Furnace, wagons, gears, horses, carts, coal, cordwood, cows, calves, bulls, steers, oxen, sheep, hogs and scraps, indented servants, 'a Negroe man called Tobe,' bar and refined iron, pigmetal and castings. At the same time, James Fullton, Thomas Smith and James Wallace, 'in Company, ironmasters,' deeded two tracts of land to Ferguson McElvaine, 'agent for said Company'.

William Smith, presumably the ironmaster who sold them Martick Forge and Furnace in the first place, went to court to collect a debt of £1,750 due him from Fullton and Wallace. Lancaster County Court issued a writ to the Sheriff 6 August 1768 to sell their property to satisfy Smith's claim. Sheriff James Webb sold a 200-acre tract of their land at the Court House door 5 November 1768.

Fullton somehow kept his share of Martick Forge and Furnace, but it never proved to be a profitable investment. In 1770 he wrote Hugh Orr of Boston that 'the Iron works that I am Concerned in is Not growing this Season occassioned throu the failure of the Iron busness in this Province, Iron Continuing So Verry Low.' As a result, Fullton and his partners attempted to dispose of their iron works by a lottery scheme, selling tickets to recoup some of their investment.[31]

From 1769 on, Fullton concentrated on shipping flour and iron to Boston for his kinsman Andrew Black and old friend Hugh Orr. He proposed to Black part ownership of a schooner 'that would Carry about 1,000 barrells flouer' so he cannot have been without resources.[32] He was certainly short of cash and wrote dunning letters to his brother John Fullton, Ephraim Campbell and Ninian Boggs in Londonderry without effect.[33] He complained to Andrew Black that 'I have near

£1000 Due to me these Severall years in and about L Derry and Cannot Recover a Shilling of it Throu some Disputes amongst themselves and one of them is now failed.'[34] The failure was his own brother, who came to Lancaster, Pennsylvania, with his family in 1773.

The last letters in the letter book refer to Fullton's efforts in the summer of 1771 to help Robert Duncan of Londonderry get established in either Baltimore, Maryland, or Alexandria, Virginia. It is not clear how much longer Fullton himself continued in business. The surviving ledgers only go to 1768 and the day books terminate in 1770. According to family tradition, he left Philadelphia with his wife and their three children, James, Samuel and Sally, when Sir William Howe and the British army advanced on the city in 1777. He spent the remainder of his life on a farm in Lower Chanceford Township, York County, Pennsylvania where he purchased in two tracts in 1760 and 1766. James Fullton died there in 1808.

His business papers went up to the attic of the farmhouse to gather dust until family members recovered them in 1938. Some pages were missing from more than one book. Dr John Farquhar Fulton of Yale University recognised the importance of the ledgers and day books and had them restored and rebound. There are five volumes in all. Two ledgers cover the period 1763-1766 and 1766-1768. The three day books are divided into 1761-1765, 1763-1766 and 1766-1770. They were given by Yale University Library to the Historical Society of York County in York, Pennsylvania. The letter book had been used as a scrap book by a nineteenth century Fulton child and suffered some damage as a result. Letters date from 1764 through 1771. It went to Dr. Harry Cuthbertson Fulton of Lancaster who encouraged Eleanore J. Fulton to make a typescript of the letters in 1942. He died at an advanced age without any immediate family. The original letter book did not apparently survive the dispersal of Dr Fulton's estate. Eleanore Fulton's transcript is in the Fulton Papers in the Lancaster County Historical Society, Lancaster, Pennsylvania and a second copy is in the Historical Society of York County.

NOTES

1 Fullton Letter Book, Library, History Society of New York County, 4 Dec. 1766.

2 S. Helen Fields, *Register of Marriages and Baptisms Performed by Rev. John Cuthbertson, Covenanter Minister, 1751-1791*. Washington D.C.: National Genealogical Society, 1934, p. 202.

3 *Pennsylvania Gazette* 17 Mar. 1763, 2 Feb. 1764.

4 Fullton Day Book, 1766-70, 18 Aug. 1768.

5 *Pennsylvania Gazette*, 23 Nov. 1758.

6 *ibid* 14 June 1759.

7 *ibid* 9 Oct. 1760.

8 *ibid* 2 April & 11 June 1761.

9 James T. Lemon, *The Best Poor Man's Country: A Genealogical Study of Early Southeastern Pennsylvania*. Baltimore, The Johns Hopkins Univ. Press, 1972, p. 125.

10 Fullton Flaxseed Account *Day Book*, 1763-66.

11 *Pennsylvania Gazette,* 25 Nov. 1762, 17 Nov. 1763.

12 Fullton Ledger A, 7-12 Dec. 1763.

13 R.J. Dickson, *Ulster Emigration to Colonial America 1718-1775*. Belfast, Ulster Historical Foundation, 1995, pp. 114n, 249.

14 *Londonderry Journal*, 1 July 1772. PRONI, MIC /60/1.

15 *Pennsylvania Gazette* 20 Dec. 1764; Fullton Letter Book 10 Dec. 1764, 9 Jan. 1765.

16 Thomas M. Doerflinger, *A Vigorous Spirit of Enterprise: Merchants and Economic Development in Revolutionary Philadelphia.* Chapel Hill, Univ. of North Carolina Press, 1986, pp. 103-4.

17 Fullton Day Book 1763-66, 19 Dec. 1765.

18 *Pennsylvania Gazette* 15 Nov. 1764.

19 *Belfast News Letter,* 26 July 1765.

20 *Belfast News Letter*, 11 Feb. 1766; Fullton Letter Book, 12 May 1766.

21 Fullton Letter Book, 22 & 27 May 1766.

22 Fullton Letter Book, 19 Dec. 1766.

23 *ibid.*

24 *Belfast News Letter*, 16 June 1767.

25 Fullton Letter Book 4 Dec. 1767.

26 Fullton Letter Book 26 Nov. 1768.

27 Fullton Letter Book 20 Feb. 1767.

28 Fulton Letter Book 7 Dec. 1768.

29 Burton Alva Konkle, *George Ryan and the Constitution of Pennsylvania 1731-1791*. Philadelphia, William J. Campbell, 1922, pp. 18-19, 23.

30 *Pennsylvania Gazette* 9 July 1767.

31 Fullton Letter Book, 3 April 1770.

32 *ibid*, 14 Nov. 1769.

33 *ibid*, 9 Dec. 1769.

34 *ibid*, 18 Dec. 1770.

THE QUALITY OF MERCY: IRISH WOMEN AND INFANTICIDE IN COLONIAL AUSTRALIA

Trevor McClaughlin

Irish women and infanticide in colonial times is a fascinating, gruesome, tragic and emotional subject. It is one which spills over into many different areas: the history of criminology and medical jurisprudence, demography, ethics and religion, literary history, women's history and, in particular, Irish women's place in Australian social history. There is such an enticing variety of questions to pursue and hypotheses to test. What motivated women, especially Irish women, to kill their own child? Were Irish women simply more likely to be caught because of their 'country Irish ways' and their 'innocence abroad'? And, crucially, were they treated leniently by the courts?

The accepted view among legal historians is that in the Australian colonies, as in Ireland and Victorian England, judges *and* juries were reluctant to convict women accused of infanticide, preferring instead the lesser charge of manslaughter or concealment of birth and the lesser penalties which these carried. The Irish author, Maurice Healy, recounts the story in his *Old Munster Circuit* in which a judge tells an infanticide mother that what he is about to say is all nonsense, and then sentences her to hang, while sending off a request for reprieve to the Lord Lieutenant of Ireland. Did this attitude also prevail in the Australian colonies? Or were *some* courts, those in Victoria for example, more willing to pursue a capital conviction than courts elsewhere? Other questions are equally engaging. For example, Kathy Laster has written in a compelling way about the challenges infanticide poses for feminist criminological theory, and about the '*arbitrary* chivalry' the male legal establishment displayed towards women's capital punishment in Victoria.

Historical demographers are interested in the part played by infanticide, concealment of birth, child abandonment, and abortion in reducing Australia's birth rate and in aiding a transition to demographic modernity. There exists a remarkable difference between the first and last decades of the nineteenth century. Portia Robinson believes that infanticide was virtually non-existent in the early period of white settlement up to 1828. By the end of the nineteenth century, however, it is a problem for historians of very significant proportions. In New South Wales between 1880 and 1909, 136 infanticide cases came before the courts; while in the same period 503 unidentified babies were taken to Sydney city morgues. In Victoria between 1885 and 1914, 125 women were charged with murder and another 85 with concealment of birth. In the same period, coronial inquests found 276 children to have been wilfully murdered and returned an open verdict on a further 300 infant corpses. Such discrepancies in the figures demonstrate that criminal records alone will not give us an accurate picture of how widespread the practice was.

As for women's history, the study of Irish women's infanticide draws attention to the vulnerability of young Irish immigrant women. It is a stark reminder of the sheer desperation of some young Irish women in their new Australian home. It emphasizes for us (if ever it needed emphasizing) the patriarchal double standards of sexual morality which existed *and* the striking contrast between the magnitude and nature of women's criminality and that of men. Infanticide draws attention to the fundamental difference between men and women's historical experience.

Regrettably it is not possible to do justice here to the full range of interesting issues this subject raises. Instead I will tell the story of a number of individuals, resurrected from the archives, and attempt to peer through one small window of their lives. In October 1854 eleven-year-old Elisabeth McCullough arrived in New South Wales from Turralish in County Down along with her three younger siblings and her father. Unfortunately her mother died on the voyage. Thirteen years later, Elisabeth McCullough appeared before Supreme Court Judge, John Fletcher Hargrave, at Bathurst Circuit Court and was charged that she did 'wilfully kill and murder her male infant on the 8th of August last'. The jury took thirty-five minutes to return a verdict of guilty of manslaughter, and the judge sentenced her to two years in Bathurst gaol with hard labour. Two things especially convicted her; the evidence of her employer, Mary Jane Green, and the evidence of the medical doctor who examined the body of her dead child.

Mary Jane Green confronted her servant Elisabeth McCullough about the changes she noticed in her appearance, and harried her until she showed her where the still warm body of her baby was, 'in a 'chamber' against the chimney 'covered over with a bag'. She pressed McCullough until she told the name of the baby's father and took it upon herself to tell what she had found, to the authorities. The medical doctor, despite a strong challenge from the defence lawyer, maintained that the infant had 'breathed for a few minutes' before dying from umbilical haemorrhage, or bleeding from the cord. The judge's notebooks throw little light on the matter, except to show that he was interested in applying the strict letter of the law. The employer, the medical doctor, the jury and the judge showed little by way of sympathy or mercy for Elisabeth McCullough, though she *was* sentenced to only two years' imprisonment.

There were thirty-seven prisoners for trial before Justice Hargrave at Bathurst Circuit Court in October 1867, a not inconsiderable number. Elisabeth McCullough from County Down was not the only Irishwoman on a child murder charge. Five days after she was sentenced, Harriet Short and Mary Williams were also found guilty of the murder of 'one female child, name unknown'. Mary Williams had come out on the *Duchess of Northumberland* in 1835 from a Foundling Hospital in Ireland. An abandoned baby herself, Mary, along with her daughter Harriet, was sentenced to death for the murder of her three week old grand-daughter whom she had 'chucked' into a well. When the jury left to consider their verdict, Mary Williams was racked 'in violent weeping and sobbing'. When the verdict was read, her daughter became hysterical. Her 'shrieks could be heard for a considerable distance from the courthouse'.

The Judge, John Hargrave, in his letter to the Governor of New South Wales, did not recommend mercy be shown to either of the women.

> With regard to the younger prisoner altho' she may be assumed to have acted throughout this sad affair as greatly under maternal influence, still her own maternal instincts must have been utterly set aside when she allowed her mother to throw the baby down the well; which was under the circumstances quite as much her own act as her mother's – Moreover the time and place selected for the murder seem to me to indicate considerable premeditation and design for concealment.

This was one case where the 'judge factor' seems to have played a considerable role. To anyone uninitiated in legal matters, such as myself, Hargrave would appear to have taken a very narrow and literal approach to the law. He rejected Harriet Short's claim that one, Charles Atkins, was the father of her child and he readily accepted Atkins's denial. This was of no importance to the matter in hand. Nor were the desperate circumstances of the two women.

'I would point out', he wrote in his letter to the Governor, explaining why he did not recommend mercy,

> that the lives of all infant children are necessarily at the mercy of the mother and her accomplices, that the facilities for secret murders of infants are very great and that the commission of this crime appears to have been much on the increase of late years especially at Bathurst. – While I fully concur in the very natural repugnance against the execution of females, – nevertheless these cases of wanton infanticide ought in my opinion rather to be classed with murders of wives by their husbands and of husbands by their wives, as domestic murders of aggravated guilt.

Fortunately the Governor did not agree. Harriet Short's death sentence was commuted to ten years' imprisonment and Mary Williams's to life. Mary Williams would have been over 60 years old when she finished serving her sentence.

Twelve years later, the presiding judge at the trial of Johanna Sullivan in Adelaide in 1879, Chief Justice Samuel Way, also had considerable influence on the outcome of the case. Johanna Sullivan, a young domestic servant, with black hair, grey eyes and protruding forehead, had arrived in Adelaide from Ireland in 1875. Four years later she was found guilty of murdering her infant child, and sentenced to death. Apparently she took her two-week-old baby boy, Patsy, to the beach at Glenelg and threw him down. He was weakened by a blow to the back of his head, it was surmised, and his mother reverently placed him in a wreath of seaweed where he later drowned.

The Chief Justice's notes clearly demonstrate how he came to the conclusion that Johanna Sullivan was guilty of murder. Samuel Way carefully drew the distinction between murder ('unlawful homicide with malice aforethought') and manslaughter.

> Did she cause the death by a blow or by throwing it into the water – murder...Was its death caused by abandoning it on the beach – then it will be murder if there was a reasonable expectation that the tide would cover up and drown it or that it would die of cold. Manslaughter if there was a contrary probability.

The Chief Justice's summing up left the jury with little alternative to a guilty verdict, but they strongly recommended her to mercy. Johanna

Sullivan had her death sentence commuted to 14 years' imprisonment with hard labour. She was released from Gladstone gaol on 18 October 1886, long before she was due for release, seemingly with a cardiac problem. A Johanna Sullivan died in South Australia sometime between 1887 and 1895 but it is unknown if this was the same Johanna Sullivan.

What is worth noting about this particular case is the wider social issues it embraced. Johanna Sullivan, just like Maggie Heffernan in Melbourne at a later date, became something of a *cause célèbre* among Adelaide's progressive social and political elite. A vigorous debate broke out in Adelaide's newspapers in the last weeks of August 1879, and continued into September. Some called her a 'human tigress' and 'female fiend', someone who wanted to get rid of her baby so she could hire herself out as a wet-nurse for monetary gain. There was much clamouring for the high moral ground. But most correspondents were aghast at the thought Johanna Sullivan might be executed and sought genuinely to understand her plight.

A Memorial, or petition, was drawn up in her favour and signed by over 2000 people at 'Glen Osmond, Glenelg, Port, Glanville, Semaphore, North and South Adelaide etc ...irrespective of lists at Banks'. B. T. Finniss drew attention to the fact Johanna may have been suffering from puerperal mania, or post-partum depression, which 'sometimes follows on childbirth, when a hatred for the child seems suddenly to arise...something', Finniss said, 'which does not appear to have struck Judge, or counsel, or Jury'. (Several witnesses attested to the fact that from the birth of the child she was in the habit of beating it.)

Former employers attested to her lunacy, or temporary aberration of mind, in an attempt to have her sentence commuted (little knowing it had already been commuted). Two of her employers were to write; 'She had not been with us two or three days when my servants objected to remain with us unless I discharged her, because they considered she was nothing less than a lunatic'– from Wm T. Dalwood of Hackney House. 'We found her...so eccentric, that after roaming about the house all night, gesticulating, moaning and disturbing everybody we were very glad when she took her departure early the next morning...at this time she most certainly was *non compos mentis*...' from David Jeffery of Avenue House, Parkside.

It is interesting that letter-writers to the press were prepared to seek an understanding of some of the things affecting women's lives. 'It is the old story', wrote Herbert Heritage, 'the real criminal – the man – escapes, while his victim is hunted out of the world'. And JHB, in the same paper, 'the public are the real murderers…it is the custom of society to utterly condemn and despise any woman who has an illegitimate child, and to reproach her with it for the whole of her life'. One week later the *Observer* put the view concisely,

> The unfortunate woman was of an excitable temperament; she had apparently been seduced and abandoned by some unprincipled and heartless scoundrel; she was penniless and friendless; her good name was lost, and her peace of mind was destroyed; she had seemingly nothing before her but the cruel alternative of a life of misery or a career of infamy so long as her unfortunate infant lived. Moreover she lacked the means of ministering to its wants, and she experienced a difficulty in providing for her own requirements. What wonder, then, that spurred on to recklessness, the distracted and miserable mother in a moment of madness sacrificed her child's life. Her guilt is not that of the hardened murderess; – hers was a deed born of utter misery and despair.

Adelaide's elite used the Sullivan case to push for legal and social reforms. One, William Liston, advocated the death penalty be done away with in cases of infanticide by the mother. He further proposed that it be made a criminal offence for the father 'to neglect to make full provision for the sustenance and care (including medical attendance) of the mother and child, for a term of say from twelve to eighteen months'. John Darling suggested in parliament that a foundling hospital be opened to destitute mothers as a place of refuge in their time of need. His suggestion was supported in the *South Australian Register* in a poem, perhaps a tad maudlin for modern tastes,

> Out in the lamp lit street, with the babe of shame at her breast, a wild-eyed woman with hurrying feet walked on in a strange unrest…behind her a father's curse, a curse and a close-shut door; madness at work in her soul… .

Many of the views expressed were replete with the prejudices and moral rectitude common at the time. Respectable South Australian society was shocked by the 'barbarity' of the crime. Yet such views should be seen in the context of the times. It also must be remembered that South Australia was the most socially progressive of the Australian colonies, the home of the Married Women's Property Act and the first to grant women the vote. As Patricia Summerling puts it, because of the Johanna Sullivan case, 'consciences were raised...to the plight of woman and the causes of such predicaments'.

In Victoria, my impression, after a brief period of research, is first, that Irish-born women were well represented among infanticide cases and, second, that Victorian courts seemed readier to pursue the death penalty than courts elsewhere. But these are very tentative claims that should be subjected to much closer scrutiny.

Between 1865 and 1892, Mary Malone (1865), Ellen Tighe (1871), Bridget Magee (1878) and Mary Fitzgerald (1892) were convicted of the gender-specific crime of infanticide. Mary Malone (or Mary Cox) from Edenderry in King's County, Ellen Tighe (or Margaret Donnelly to give her her real name) and Mary Fitzgerald from County Kerry, to a greater or lesser degree, fit the stereotype of the young Irish servant girl, without friends in the world, abandoned by their seducer, naïve, frightened and overwrought and, most likely suffering from a temporary aberration of the mind, murdered their babies and made a botched job of covering up their crimes.

Mary Malone was 19 years old when she arrived in Melbourne in 1860. Shortly after, in August 1862, she sent home £18 passage money for her sisters, Bridget and Kate. Among the pleas for commutation of her death sentence was the fact she was 'a good girl', 'steady, kind and gentle' to her employer's children. Nonetheless in February 1865, the jury found her guilty (Mary's baby had been found strangled with a piece of calico bound tightly round its neck), but made 'a strong recommendation to mercy on the grounds of youth and her deserted condition'.

Ellen Tighe was 'an exceedingly timid girl'. After her conviction in 1871 it was found she had 'given all her money to [a] Mr Shepherd for her defence'. Yet at her trial she was undefended. A handkerchief and strings of an apron were found round the neck of her dead male child found in the cesspool of a neighbour's house in Melbourne. The jury's verdict was 'Guilty – with a strong recommendation to mercy on grounds of the circumstantial nature of the evidence'.

Mary Fitzgerald was also treated leniently. She was a young domestic servant from Kerry who drowned her baby in a puddle of water near Wangaratta in 1892. Among the pleas on her behalf were those of former employers; she was 'a temperate hard-working girl', 'a hard-working honest girl', 'very affectionate of their two children' who 'refused on several occasions to kill a fowl'. Residents from Benalla and district, in a petition organised by the Benalla branch of the Women's Christian Temperance Union, and residents from Wangaratta and district wrote to the Governor of Victoria claiming Mary Fitzgerald was 'deserted by a man who deceived her and without friends or money, put an end to a life in a fit of despair and when in a state of madness'. Even the sentencing judge, Mr Justice Hood, wrote in her favour to the Victorian Executive Council, arguing strongly that a sentence of three to five years would be appropriate. Mary was the classic example of the young unmarried servant girl whose case was met sympathetically by public opinion and the Victorian legal system.

Bridget Magee (nee Edwards) from County Clare did not fit the stereotype so easily. She was found guilty of being an accessory to the murder of her new-born child. Her husband, Robert Magee, a Presbyterian from Antrim, was found drowned in 1876 in a dam near Bendigo Creek in what police regarded as suspicious circumstances. Soon after, Bridget's lover, Peter Kane, moved in with her on her farm and there was a baby born eleven months later whom Peter Kane decided to murder. Bridget's child, 13 year old Margaret, the eldest of her seven children, gave evidence at the trial in 1878, 'I heard some conversation between my mother and Kane, they were talking in Irish, I did not understand what they [then] said. I heard Peter Kane say in English, something about drowning baby and my mother said "Faith then you wont".' This statement was the reason the jury recommended Bridget to mercy. But to no avail. Bridget was sentenced to 15 years' hard labour and Peter Kane to 20 years, the first three years in irons. Bridget's seven children went to the nuns at Abbotsford. It is unknown if she was reunited with her seven children when she was released early from gaol in 1889.

From the selection of cases reported here, there are a number of tentative conclusions to draw. I, personally, would be wary of providing a simple answer to the question of what motivated Irish infanticides. To argue strongly in favour of biological determinism, *post-partum* depression, for example, or economic and social determinism – poverty and hardship or the crushing burden of shame – is to do injustice to the complexities involved. We do not know the full story of Elisabeth McCullough or Ellen Tighe. Nor do we fully understand the nature of the relationship between Harriet Short and her husband Albert. We are only slightly better off when it comes to understanding the relationship with her mother. Regrettably we only ever come into contact with infanticides indirectly, the subaltern class generally, through some biased intermediary such as court records, and then, only temporarily.

It does not appear that Irish-born women were over-represented among convicted infanticides in colonial Australia, certainly not in New South Wales and South Australia. Their relatively larger number in Victoria was as much a consequence of the disproportionate number of single Irish-born women who immigrated between 1848 and 1870 than anything else.

Another interpretation is that their rate of conviction had something to do with the Victorian legal system, or anti-Irish prejudice in the courts. Irish women were well represented at the lower end of the social scale and for this reason were likely to have been brought to trial. But their Irishness or ethnicity was not an issue in any of the cases reviewed above, at least not publicly so.

Initially, my impression was that Victorian courts were more likely to pursue the death penalty in cases of infanticide than courts elsewhere, courts in other colonies being quicker to acknowledge how difficult it was to *prove* that a new-born baby had actually been born alive. This difference, I thought, was the result of a more liberal judiciary in New South Wales, Queensland and South Australia. This view, however, is not supported by the examples examined today. The least liberal judge was Justice Hargrave at the NSW trials in Bathurst in 1867. In the Victorian cases, police, medical doctors, juries and judges all displayed, at some stage, an element of mercy in their dealings with Irish women accused of infanticide. Mary Malone, Ellen Tighe, Mary Fitzgerald and even Bridget Magee were all recommended to mercy by the juries who convicted them. It might have been a different story had their crimes been committed slightly later, in the depressed and depressing 1890s, when women *were* executed for child-murder.

Finally, it would be interesting to pursue the significance of this gender-specific crime, infanticide, for the history of Irish women in colonial Australia. The crime might illustrate to us the sheer desperation of some young Irish women in their harsh new world. Yet rather than 'victims' these women might *also* be seen as 'strong' women who took it 'upon themselves to determine their own fertility'. Was there an increase in arrests and sentencing of infanticides between the 1850s and the 1890s? Was infanticide only the tip of a mountain of reproductive related crimes, especially in the decade before Federation?

Does infanticide also underscore the patriarchal double standard of sexual morality? Only in the Johanna Sullivan case did anyone suggest she should not have been alone in the dock. Infanticide, some would argue, demonstrates the fundamental difference between men and women's historical experience. If we deconstruct the language of our texts – newspaper accounts, police reports, trial records, judges' notebooks – and analyse the cultural anxieties of the times to 'represent' our women themselves we could write a very different story. But that is for another time.

MANDARINS ON THE HILL: HEADS OF THE NORTHERN IRELAND CIVIL SERVICE 1921-2001

Sir Kenneth Bloomfield

The recent sad death of Sir William Ewart Bell, who served as the ninth head of the Northern Ireland Civil Service from 1979-1984, reminds us that this office, currently held by Mr G. D. Loughran as its thirteenth occupant, has now been in existence for almost eighty years. It may be timely, then, to give some account of the thirteen men (and, unfortunately, so far no women) who have served as Heads of the Northern Ireland Civil Service over some eight decades.

The first three holders of the post were born in the nineteenth century. When Sir Ernest Clark took up office, as the first servant of the infant Northern Ireland Government, in November 1921, he had already behind him a record of public service reaching as far back as 1904 when, after studies at the Bar and a call to the Middle Temple in 1894, he had been seconded for service in the Cape Colony of South Africa. On his return to Britain, he served in positions of increasing seniority in the British Civil Service, acting (when an Assistant Secretary at the Board of Inland Revenue) as Secretary to the Royal Commission on Income Tax in 1919 and 1920, before moving to the Irish Office as an Assistant Under Secretary in 1920. After partition, he opted to throw in his lot with the newly established government of Northern Ireland, becoming the first Secretary to the Ministry of Finance and (by right of that position) Head of the Northern Ireland Civil Service in November 1921. After leaving the Northern Ireland Civil Service in March 1925, his only later official contact with Northern Ireland was to serve for a time in the 1930s as a member of the Joint Exchequer Board, the body designated to act as 'referee' between the Northern Ireland Ministry of Finance and HM Treasury in the event of disagreement about the finances of Northern Ireland. He held various directorships among them the London Underground, Martins Bank and Harland & Wolff, and served as Governor of Tasmania from 1933 to 1945.

Clark's successor, after serving for less than three and a half years, was to be Lieutenant Colonel Sir Wilfrid Spender, previously the first Secretary of the Northern Ireland Cabinet. He had been a professional soldier of some distinction and ability. He had been commissioned into the Royal Artillery in 1897, passed Staff College at Camberley, taken the Royal Navy War Course and served on the General Staff and a sub-committee of the Committee of Imperial Defence. However in 1913, being opposed in principle to what he saw as the prospective imposition of partition on Ulster, he retired from the army to serve on the Headquarter staff of the then Ulster Volunteer Force. On the outbreak of the First World War he returned to the Colours, served as a general staff officer and was awarded the Military Cross, the Distinguished Service Order and four mentions in dispatches. After the armistice, Spender was chosen by Earl Hague to organise the officers' *friend branch* at the Ministry of Pensions and to serve on the committee which led to the establishment of the British Legion. But Spender was not to remain for long in Whitehall; he had become personally close to James Craig, who was to become Northern Ireland's first Prime Minister, and agreed to return to Ulster to re-raise and command the Ulster Volunteer Force, which was transmuted into the Ulster Special Constabulary. It was, therefore, a distinctly political public servant who was chosen by Craig in 1921 to be his first Cabinet Secretary. Appointed to succeed Ernest Clark at the Ministry of Finance on 1 April 1925, he was to remain in that post until his retirement at the end of June 1944, aged 67. He died in 1960 at the age of 84.

The third post-holder was to be Sir William Dalgeish Scott, a graduate of Edinburgh University and a member of the English Bar who had joined the Board of Inland Revenue in 1910 and became involved in Irish affairs on joining the staff of the Chief Secretary for Ireland in 1920. When Ireland was partitioned he, along with many Protestant civil servants who had worked in Dublin, chose to come north to serve in the administration of the new government of Northern Ireland. Appointed Assistant Secretary at the Ministry of Finance in 1921, he was promoted in 1924 to be Secretary of the Ministry of Commerce, at the exceptionally early age of 34, and served there for almost 20 years until 1944. While serving at the Ministry of Commerce, he had become involved in various other activities closely related to its responsibilities: as the Industrial Insurance Commissioner from 1924 to 1944, and as Chairman of the Electricity Commissioners for

Northern Ireland from 1924 to 1931. The outbreak of the Second World War had brought him into the centre of wartime planning and control in the Province, as Core Controller (1939-42), Regional Representative of the Board of Trade (1940-44) and Regional Controller at different times for the Ministries of Supply, Production and Aircraft Production. Such was the record of the man who on 1 July 1944 succeeded Sir Wilfrid Spender as Secretary of the Ministry of Finance and Head of the Northern Ireland Civil Service. In these capacities he was to serve for almost nine years, until his retirement at the end of March 1953 at the age of 62. He was, however, to pursue a most active retirement until his death in October 1966 at the age of 75. In the public sphere he served on the Committee on Teachers' Salaries in 1954 and as a member of an Economic Commission to Malta in 1956-57. He also acted as chairman of various bodies, including the governors of Ashley House School, the Ulster Scot Historical Society, the Central Council of the Irish Linen Industry and the Linen Industry Research Association. Scott was in turn succeeded by the first post-holder born in the twentieth century (September 1902), Sir Douglas Alexander Earsman Harkness. Educated at the High School of Newport, Monmouthshire and at the University of Glasgow (where he took a first in Economic Science in 1923) Harkness had joined the Northern Ireland Ministry of Agriculture in 1924 and was to remain there until 1952, becoming the Secretary of the Department in 1948. In 1952, however, anticipating Scott's prospective retirement, Harkness joined the Ministry of Finance as its Second Secretary, and was therefore in place to succeed on his retirement at the beginning of April 1953. Some incompatibility between Harkness and the then Finance Minister Terence O'Neill led to his 'sideways move' to be Economic Adviser to the government of Northern Ireland in 1962 and to his retirement from the service in 1963, the year of O'Neill's preferment to the premiership. To much surprise, Harkness in retirement undertook a political career, and was to serve as a Unionist Councillor for Clifton Ward in the Belfast City Council from 1967 to 1973.

These four men – Clark, Spender, Scott and Harkness – account for approximately half of the total existence of the office and the Northern Ireland Civil Service, and were responsible for leadership of that Service through the difficult pre-war, war-time and immediate post-war periods. With the exception of Harkness, all of them had served in government departments outside Northern Ireland before joining the Northern Ireland Civil Service: Clark and Scott in the Inland Revenue and Spender in the Ministry of Pensions. With the exception of Spender, all of them were graduates of universities in Great Britain: Clark at London (King's College), Scott at Edinburgh and the London School of Economics and Harkness at Glasgow. It is striking that the Northern Ireland Civil Service experienced only four heads in the first 40 years of its existence, compared with nine in the next 40, but this reflected the particularly lengthy tenure of Spender (more than 19 years), while both Scott and Harkness served for more than eight years each.

The successor to Harkness in September 1961 was Sir Richard Frederick Roberts Dunbar, born in May 1900 in the middle of the Boer War and carrying through life a forename celebrating the eminent General of that war, Roberts. Previously known familiarly throughout the Service as 'Bobs' Dunbar, he chose to use after his Knighthood in 1964 his first Christian name of Richard. Dunbar was the first Irishman to head the Northern Ireland Civil Service, but his origins had been in the South, where he had been born, went to school at Mountjoy in Dublin and joined the Civil Service in 1919. In 1922, however, he transferred to the Northern Ireland Ministry of Finance, but much of his subsequent career was at the Ministry of Home Affairs, where he served as Secretary before promotion to the Headship at the Ministry of Finance. Already 61 at the time of his appointment, he was killed in a road accident not long after his retirement in 1965. An interesting feature of his tenure was that while the leading civil servant in Belfast was a Dubliner, his closest equivalent in Dublin (though not formally recognised as Head of the Irish Civil Service) was a son of Rostrevor in County Down, the widely respected T.K. (Ken) Whitaker.

It was not, therefore, until more than 43 years had passed that the Northern Ireland Civil Service was to be led by a native son, Sir Cecil Joseph Bateman, educated at the Methodist College in Belfast and a graduate of the Queen's University in that city. Cecil Bateman had joined the Northern Ireland Civil Service in 1927 as a young man of seventeen, but like many of his generation saw his talents flourish during the challenge of the Second World War, in which he served with the Royal Artillery, returning to duty as 'Major Bateman' with a renewed confidence. Thereafter he rose steadily through the ranks, serving as Director of Establishments (effectively the Personnel

Manager of the Service) at the Ministry of Finance from 1958 to 1963, and as Secretary to the (O'Neill) Cabinet and Clerk of the Privy Council from 1963 to 1965 before his appointment to the highest post on 1 April 1965. Having been a party, as Cabinet Secretary, to the historic O'Neill-Lemass meeting at the beginning of 1965, Bateman was to face the demanding task of leading the Northern Ireland Civil Service through the earliest period of civil strife in the late 1960s and the deepening involvement of the United Kingdom government in the affairs of the Province. After this retirement in 1970, Bateman was to become chairman of the shipping company G. Heyn & Sons and a director of the Nationwide Building Society, of Allied Irish Bank and Allied Irish Investment Bank.

Bateman was succeeded by the last holder of the office (so far) not born in Northern Ireland. Sir David Charles Beresford Holden, educated at Rossall School in Lancashire and at King's College, Cambridge, had entered the Northern Ireland Civil Service in 1937, and served throughout the Second World War in the Royal Artillery. Known in the immediate post-war period as 'Major Holden', he rose steadily through the ranks at the Ministry of Finance, succeeding Noel Cox as the principal negotiator with H M Treasury about the arcane financial arrangements of Northern Ireland under the Government of Ireland Act 1920. He succeeded Bateman as Permanent Secretary at the Ministry and Head of the Civil Service on 1 July 1970, and inherited the onerous responsibility of seeing the Service through the turbulent transition from the last days of the Stormont government to the onset of Direct Rule in 1972.

The arrival on the scene of William Whitelaw as the first Secretary of State for Northern Ireland brought with it a significant change in his responsibilities. While retaining titular secretaryship at the Ministry of Finance, he left Parliament Buildings for Stormont Castle, with the Ministry's Second Secretary, Robert Kidd, taking over the day-to-day administration of the department. At Stormont Castle, Holden was to be the most senior member (together with Sir Harold Black and Kenneth Bloomfield of the former Cabinet Secretariat) of a triumvirate of Northern Ireland civil servants embedded into the headquarters staff of the new Northern Ireland Office. In this role Holden chaired an important Future Policy Group, which was heavily involved in contingency for the return of devolved government, and with

Bloomfield joined the United Kingdom delegation to the Sunningdale Conference held in late 1973, leading up to the establishment on 1 January 1974 of the short-lived 'power-sharing' Executive. During that Executive's brief tenure of office, Holden acted as the joint Chairman from Northern Ireland of the official steering group concerned with the functions and responsibilities of a potential Council of Ireland. After the collapse of the Executive in May 1974, Holden returned to his post at the Ministry of Finance, combining his Headship of the Northern Ireland Civil Service with that position until his retirement at the end of June 1976. Thereafter he was to serve as Director of the Ulster Office (Northern Ireland's 'shop window' in London) in 1976-77.

Holden was then succeeded as Head by his deputy at the Ministry of Finance, Sir Robert Hill Kidd, a native Ulsterman and the first of three old boys of the Royal Belfast Academical Institution to hold the post between 1976 and 1997. Born in 1918, Kidd had studied at Trinity College Dublin before serving in the Royal Ulster Rifles and the Intelligence Corps from 1941 to 1946. Entering the Northern Ireland Civil Service in 1947 he had a distinguished career in the Ministry of Finance, culminating in his appointment to be Second Secretary there from 1969 to 1976. From the inception of the Northern Ireland Civil Service, the two most senior posts in the Service had been recognised to be the Secretaryships respectively of the Ministry of Finance and of the Cabinet. All holders of both posts could expect in due course to receive the honour of a Knighthood. Clearly the Headship of the Northern Ireland Civil Service could in theory be combined with either of these posts, but in practice had from the outset been brigaded with the Secretaryship of Finance as the most senior department. However, after the collapse of the 1974 Executive, and with little confidence in the early restoration of devolution, the post of Cabinet Secretary (or, in 1974, Secretary of the Executive) ceased to exist. There was, on the other hand, perceived to be real benefit in incorporating into the Secretary of State's central secretariat at Stormont Castle as Senior Northern Ireland Civil Servant alongside his Whitehall colleagues. This led, on Robert Kidd's appointment, to the decision to separate the post of Head of the Northern Ireland Civil Service from the Secretaryship at the Ministry of Finance, with Kidd and his successors serving essentially as the Secretary of State's most senior local adviser.

After his retirement in 1979 Kidd took on a wide range of public and private sector appointments, including the important role of pro-Chancellor and Chairman of the Council at the New University of Ulster, where his powers of diplomacy were productively engaged in the merger with the Ulster Polytechnic to create in 1985 the University of Ulster.

It was perhaps fitting, in view of the historic sporting and other rivalries, that a son of RBAI was to be succeeded by a son of the Methodist College, Sir William Ewart Bell. Born in 1924, and a son of the Manse, Bell had taught briefly at Cheltenham College after graduating from Wadham College, Oxford. Entering the Northern Ireland Civil Service in 1948 he rapidly made his name both as a skilful administrator and as a rugby footballer (for Ulster and Ireland). Initially posted to the Ministry of Health and Local Government, he went on to hold positions of increasing importance at the Ministry of Commerce, culminating in a term as its Permanent Secretary from 1973 to 1976. After three further years as Secretary at the Ministry of Finance from 1976 to 1979, his appointment to succeed Kidd was widely expected. In the middle of his term, however, there was to be a further significant adjustment in the role and status of the post-holder; in 1981 it was decided that the Head of the Northern Ireland Civil Service should carry the parallel appointment of Second Permanent Under Secretary of State of the Northern Ireland Office, thus giving the holder of the two offices an accepted position at the 'top table' in Whitehall, including attendance at the regular weekly meetings chaired by the Secretary to the Cabinet, and at the autumn colloquies of the service's 'College of Cardinals' at Sunningdale. After this retirement in 1984, Ewart Bell occupied positions of growing importance on the world of international rugby football. This post-retirement career reached its apotheosis when, as Chairman of the International Rugby Federation World Cup, he stood alongside Nelson Mandela in South Africa in 1995 as the cherished trophy was presented to Francois Pienaar, the Springbok captain.

While Bell's succession to Kidd had been widely foreseen and virtually taken for granted, those concerned with the succession after his retirement in 1984 faced a much more difficult and invidious decision. Serving at Finance was W. G. H. Quigley, a man of unrivalled intellectual grasp and enormous creative energy, who would most certainly have made a most distinguished and successful Head of the Northern Ireland

Civil Service. Had the emphasis at the time been primarily on the social and economic rather than upon the constitutional and political, he might well have been expected to succeed Bell. On the other hand Kenneth Percy Bloomfield, then Permanent Secretary at the Department of Economic Development, had particularly strong credentials in the political and constitutional areas and it was almost certainly his extensive experience in those areas that led to his appointment to succeed Bell in November 1984.

Bloomfield was the second Instonian (after Robert Kidd) to serve in the post. He had read Modern History at St Peter's Hall, Oxford after his time at RBAI, and entered the Northern Ireland Civil Service in 1952 through the Method One (Open Examination) mode of entry to the Administrative Class. Posted first of all to the Ministry of Finance, he was to serve there (from 1956 to 1959) as Private Secretary to three successive Finance Ministers; Brian Maginness, George B. Hanna and Terence O'Neill. From 1960 to 1963 he had worked in New York as Deputy Director of the British Industrial Development Office, returning to Belfast after the appointment of O'Neill as Prime Minister, to serve first as Assistant and then as Deputy Secretary of the Cabinet until the onset of Direct Rule. As already explained, he then joined Sir David Holden and Sir Harold Black in Secretary of State William Whitelaw's Stormont Castle team, and took part in the Sunningdale Conference before appointment on 1 of January 1974 as Secretary of the Executive (and thus effectively Cabinet Secretary to the new power-sharing regime). After its collapse, and a brief period of further work for the Northern Ireland Office, he entered in 1975 upon a series of departmental appointments: first at the Department of Housing, Local Government and Planning (with responsibility for merging it with the Department of the Environment under the latter name), and then with the Department of Commerce (and, after its merger with the Department of Manpower services, the new Department of Economic Development). At the time of succeeding Ewart Bell as Head of the Northern Ireland Civil Service and second Permanent Under Secretary of the Northern Ireland Office, the negotiations leading to the Anglo-Irish Agreement of 1985 were well under way. Although he played no part in these negotiations, Bloomfield was from late 1985 onwards heavily involved in their aftermath, including discussions with the United States authorities about the creation of an International Fund for Ireland,

and efforts to move forward from the political boycott imposed post-Agreement by the Unionist parties. In September 1988 Bloomfield and his family were fortunate to escape death or injury when their home at Crawfordsburn in Co. Down was the target of an explosives attack by the IRA. After his retirement in April 1991 Bloomfield took on a wide range of public and private sector responsibilities – as the Northern Ireland National Governor of the BBC; as Chairman of the Northern Ireland Higher Education Council; as Victims Commissioner for Northern Ireland; and in inquiries into subjects as varied as the governmental arrangements in Jersey and the procedures for appointing bishops in the Church of England.

On Bloomfield's retirement in April 1991 his successor, both as Head of the Northern Ireland Civil Service and as Second PUS of the Northern Ireland Office, was David Fell, who had also been his successor at the Department of Economic Development. Born in January 1943, Fell was thus 48 years of age at the time of his appointment and was at that time the youngest man ever to occupy the most senior post. Once again the appointee was a son of the Royal Belfast Academical Institution, from which he had progressed to Queen's University Belfast where he gained a First. He was not an immediate entrant to the Civil Service, gaining experience successively as a Sales Manager for Rank Hovis McDougall, as a teacher and as a research associate, before entering the Northern Ireland Civil Service in 1969. His initial service there, from 1969 to 1972, was at the Department of Agriculture, but the central core of his career was devoted to the economic areas of government, first at the Department of Commerce and then at its successor Department of Economic Development where he became an Under Secretary in 1982 and to which he returned for a term as Permanent Secretary from 1984 to 1991. Between 1982 and 1984 he remained in another capacity at the centre of economic development as a Deputy Chief Executive at the Industrial Development Board. Having received a CB in 1990 he was to be advanced to KCB as Head of the Service in 1995. Much of his period in the most senior office was to be devoted to the efforts to achieve a political settlement in Northern Ireland, first under John Major's conservative government and thereafter under Tony Blair's labour administration. In 1997, however, and still well short of the statutory retirement age from the civil service, Fell decided to resign to pursue a business career. Becoming first of all Chairman of the Northern Bank, and serving on the Boards of a number of other companies, Fell's combination of economic and business experience with an understanding of the world of public affairs clearly made him a substantial asset to a number of private sector organisations.

In a reversal of the more normal expectations, Fell was succeeded by an older man, John Laughlin Semple, who had been born in August 1940. Semple was to be the first Head of the Northern Ireland Civil Service to emerge from another of Northern Ireland's long-established grammar schools, Campbell College in Belfast. Thereafter he took an MA at Cambridge University (Corpus Christi College) followed by a BSc (Econ) from London University. Having been successful in the contest for entry to the Administrative Class of the Civil Service, Semple opted initially to join the Home Civil Service, to which he was appointed in 1961. In the following year, however, he decided to transfer to the Northern Ireland Civil Service, where he served across a wide range of departments, health and local government, community relations, health and social services and finance. A central part of his career was his work at the Ministry of Development and its successor Department of the Environment between 1972 and 1983, where he made very significant contributions to the development of housing and planning policies. However in 1983, in the rank of Under Secretary, he was transferred to the Department of Finance, and in 1988 succeeded as Permanent Secretary there Dr (as he then was) George Quigley, who like David Fell was to leave the NICS early to take on a bank chairmanship, in his case at the Ulster Bank. In 1997 Semple succeeded Fell as Head of the Northern Ireland Civil Service, but the duties and responsibilities of the post were at the time under review, and the new appointee was not initially appointed also to be the Second PUS at the Northern Ireland Office, and remained for the time being in charge at the Department of Finance. In all of this there was a real danger that this hiatus would create an impression of attempts to distance the Northern Ireland Civil Service from efforts to secure political development; however in 1998 this further designation was accorded to him. Inevitably, though, Semple's position in the scheme of things changed again following the onset of the devolutionary arrangements provided for in the Good Friday Agreement. And thus Semple's final functional role from 1992 until his retirement in the following year was to act as the first Secretary of the Executive Committee (or Cabinet) of Northern Ireland. Having been appointed CB in 1993, Semple was promoted KCB in 2000.

To complete this roster, since August 2000 the Headship of the Northern Ireland Civil Service has been in the capable hands of Gerry Loughran. Educated at St Malachy's College and Queen's University Belfast, Loughran was the first Roman Catholic in almost 80 years to hold the position. He had entered the Northern Ireland Civil Service after experience in a family business and as a university teacher. As Deputy Secretary at the Department of the Environment responsible for Town and Country Planning and Urban Regeneration, Loughran had contributed significantly to the regeneration of Belfast and Derry city centres and to initiatives including Laganside. He remains at the time of writing the professional Head of some 29,000 civil servants and acts as Head of the Office of the First Minister and Deputy First Minister and as Secretary to the Northern Ireland Executive.

It will be seen, then, that these thirteen post-holders came from varying backgrounds. Some had been lifelong civil servants, while others had entered the career after gaining experience elsewhere. A minority had served in Whitehall as well as Stormont. Four of them held the office of Second PUS at the Northern Ireland Office alongside the Headship of the Northern Ireland Civil Service. Clark, Spender, Scott, Harkness, Dunbar and Bateman held their posts only under the old Government of Northern Ireland, and Kidd, Bloomfield and Fell only under Direct Rule, working to successive Secretaries of State. Holden was to experience the transitions from the government of Northern Ireland to Direct Rule, the brief return to devolution under the power-sharing Executive of 1974, and the resumption of Direct Rule thereafter. Semple experienced the transition from Direct Rule to the new Northern Ireland Executives, whereas Loughran has had to cope with the arrangements for devolved government both when active and in suspense.

The first nine post-holders, from Clark to Bell, either held the Headship alongside the Secretaryship of the Department of Finance or moved into the post directly from that position. Amongst their four successors, only Semple moved into the office from the Department of Finance, while the other three – Bloomfield, Fell and Loughran – all moved on from the Department of Economic Development. In a sense, the trend had been similar to that in Whitehall, where Heads of the Home Civil Service were at one time rooted in the Treasury, whereas in more recent times the Head has been Secretary to the Cabinet and effectively the Prime Minister's most senior official adviser. In an age emphasing 'joined up government', the demand has been for an effective conductor of the bureaucratic orchestra rather than a virtuoso on a solo instrument.

It will be seen, too, that the initial character of the Service was very much conditioned by the practices and personalities of Whitehall, so that it was as late as 1965 before an indubitably native Ulsterman, in Cecil Bateman, was to hold the post. Thereafter, with the exception of David Holden, those appointed were the products of Northern Ireland's well-known grammar schools; three (Kidd, Bloomfield and Fell) from the Royal Belfast Academical Institution, two (Bateman and Bell) from the Methodist College, Belfast, one (Semple) from Campbell College and one (Loughran) from St Malachy's College. The non-Ulstermen had been educated in places as diverse as Winchester, Harrow, Rossall, Mountjoy School in Dublin and the High School of Newport, Monmouthshire. Many of the post-holders continued to lead active and busy lives after their retirement from the Northern Ireland Civil Service.

LIBERALISM UNDER THE UNION: THREE GENERATIONS OF AN IRISH LIBERAL FAMILY

J. L. McCracken

The bicentenary in 2001 of the union between Great Britain and Ireland, which came into effect when the Act of Union was introduced in 1801, provides an appropriate occasion for recalling the role of an Irish family whose prominence in public life over three generations as avowed and dedicated liberals coincided almost exactly with the 119 years that the union lasted. The Porters were not adherents of one of Ireland's leading socio-political faiths. In the heart of Dublin there is a pub called 'The Flowing Tide'. The name has nothing to do with any product it dispenses; it was adopted in the latter half of the nineteenth century by the then owner from a speech Gladstone made in which he claimed that the flowing tide of liberal opinion would make home rule a certainty. But liberalism was never a flowing tide in Ireland; what Gladstone discerned in the early 1880s was rather a temporary spate in a placid stream which was soon to dry up almost entirely.

After all the drama which accompanied its making the union brought about little change in Irish parliamentary representation except, of course, by reducing the number of Irish MPs from 300 to 100. But those who survived were the same men, or the same sort of men, as had sat in the Irish parliament during its period of office, 1692-1800. Indeed, of all the members who represented Ireland from 1801 to 1920 fewer than six per cent came from families who had not had members in the Irish parliament. So they blended into the Westminster pattern, the more so as those who had opposed the union made no attempt to carry on opposition or found an Irish party, some of them even accepting office. Some became absorbed in the British parties or groups and many simply sided with the party in power. So the whig or liberal party had ascendancy support in post-union Ireland from the beginning and retained it into the 1860s or 1870s, but it also had, especially in the north, non-conformist middle-class and tenant farmer adherents and periodic catholic good will or active backing when some tenet of liberalism was acceptable to the catholic majority. Thus in the O'Connell era liberals' support for catholic emancipation won them catholic goodwill and liberal non-conformists, like catholics, benefited from O'Connell's accord with Melbourne's liberal government.

As Gladstone became increasingly concerned with Irish problems, the popularity with the catholic majority of aspects of his policy, like disestablishment of the Church of Ireland and land reform, was reflected in an upsurge of electoral support for liberal candidates. That the catholic majority's support for liberalism was selective, however, became evident when the ballot act of 1872 and the parliamentary reforms of the 1880s effectively enfranchised them and they opted overwhelmingly for Parnell and nationalism. On the liberal side there had been evidence of reservations as well; O'Connell lost the backing of a sizable number of Irish liberal MPs when he took up repeal and disestablishment so upset the earl of Charlemont that he inaugurated an annual ritual of tarring the heads of the busts of liberal heroes like Gladstone and Bright with which he had filled his house in the heyday of his liberalism. Gladstone's adoption of home rule put paid to liberalism as an independent political force in Irish politics; henceforth it survived only among pressure groups and individuals. The record of the Porter family's loyalty to liberalism reveals much about the nature and role of the movement in Ireland.

The first of the family to attain prominence in liberal circles in Ireland was Revd William Porter, the son of a tenant farmer near Omagh, Co. Tyrone. Like all aspirants to the ministry of the presbyterian church in his day he went to Glasgow for his university education because Ireland's only university, Trinity College, Dublin, was an exclusively Anglican institution. For his theological training he moved to the university of Edinburgh because his father, a strict Calvinist, had heard disturbing reports about the unorthodox views of some of the Glasgow professors. After two years in Edinburgh Porter came home qualified to take charge of a congregation. It was two years before he found one. The delay may have been due in part to the disturbed state of the country, for it was the time of the disarming of Ulster and the 1798 rebellion, but primarily it was due to the heterodox views which Porter had absorbed in Scotland, in spite of his father's precaution. Eventually, after a unanimous vote of approval he was ordained in charge of the Limavady, Co. Londonderry congregation on 1 August 1799 and there he remained for the rest of his life.

Unlike many presbyterians and some presbyterian ministers, neither Revd William Porter nor his family was involved in the United Irish conspiracy or the rebellion. His brother James who inherited the home farm was an officer in the pro-government yeomanry and Porter himself was chaplain to the Limavady corps of volunteers at the time of the threatened French invasion in 1805. But if his political loyalty was beyond question his doctrinal orthodoxy was suspect among many of his fellow ministers. Yet he was so respected for his ability and integrity and so well known because of his long probation period when he had preached to many congregations that, when the clerkship of the general synod of Ulster fell vacant in 1816, he was elected to the office. In addition to a salary of £50 a year the office brought him considerable influence and prominence but it in no way altered his convictions. Porter was at the heart of the controversy which escalated in the 1820s between the orthodox majority, or Old Light party, and the Arian or New Light group within the presbyterian church who, in addition to having various heterodox doctrines on the Trinity, were opposed to a too rigid definition of belief, such as the enforced subscription to the Westminster Confession of Faith, insisted on by the orthodox party. His increasingly outspoken assertions of his belief made him the target of attack by the orthodox majority. Repeated attempts were made to oust him from the clerkship and when a split in the church came in 1830 he and his congregation were among the seceders. In May 1830 he was elected first moderator of the remonstrant synod, the governing body of the unitarians, and in September 1831 he was appointed clerk of the synod, an office which he held till his death in 1843.

Like other New Light leaders Porter was liberal in his politics. He and his fellow non-subscriber, Revd Henry Montgomery, were prominent advocates of catholic emancipation, the most contentious issue of the day, and Porter was presented with a silver service in appreciation of his support.

All of Revd William Porter's family adhered to his New Light principles but the two who figured most prominently in public life were his two sons by his first wife, John Scott and William. The elder, John Scott Porter, followed his father into the ministry of the unitarian church, as did two other sons subsequently. He was educated at Belfast Academical Institution, regarded as a hot-bed of heterodoxy by the Old Light majority, and after obtaining its general certificate which was accepted by nonconformists as the equivalent of the M.A. degree of a Scottish university, he was installed as minister of the Carter Lane congregation in the City of London in 1826. A member of his congregation with whom he formed a lifelong friendship was Joseph Chamberlain of Milk Street, head of a long-established family firm of shoemakers, a member of the Cordwainers' Company and father of Joseph Chamberlain, the radical statesman of the next generation. In addition to his pastoral duties Porter and another minister conducted a school at Islington Green. Among their pupils were two subsequent lords mayor of London, Alderman William Lawrence, MP and Sir James Clarke Lawrence, Bart., MP, and R. Brocklehurst, MP for Macclesfield. Dion Boucicault the dramatist was another of their pupils.

After six years in London Porter returned to Belfast as minister of First Presbyterian Congegration, Rosemary Street, Belfast. Among those who attended his installation was William Crolly, Catholic bishop of Down and Conor, who had been vigorously supported by Porter's father and Revd Henry Montgomery during the catholic emancipation campaign. For the rest of his life Porter was one of Belfast's most prominent citizens. His oratorical talents, sound scholarship and fair-mindedness won him a great reputation in an age when doctrinal controversy was a popular obsession. He made his reputation early in his career in a great debate on unitarianism with a leading church of Ireland protagonist, Revd Daniel Bagot, later dean of Dromore; it attracted a large audience who paid a substantial entrance fee, lasted for four days and the published proceedings ran into four editions. Porter's congregation was so pleased with his performance that they presented him with £1,000. He was also a prolific writer, contributing articles to theological journals, editing two of them at various times, and publishing over thirty books or pamphlets on religious moral and social issues, including a substantial work entitled *Principles of textual criticism*. His interests were not solely parochial; when the bishop of Natal, John William Colenso, precipitated a storm in Britain and South Africa by questioning the literal truth of the Pentateuch, Porter contributed a series of articles to the *Christian Unitarian* in which, while criticising some of the arguments, he concluded that the bishop's views were irrefutable. He was also involved in preparing students for the ministry of the unitarian church as professor of theology and of Hebrew to the association of Irish non-subscribing presbyterians. He was a strong opponent of denominational control of the national schools, advocated the preservation of the Irish language, was a member of the Belfast literary society, and was on the committee of various charitable organisations and of the society for the prevention of cruelty to animals.

Porter did not involve himself in political issues, apart from national education which had ecclesiastical implications, but his political sympathies were in harmony with those of Frank Dalzell Finlay who was married to his sister, Mary Ann. Finlay founded the *Northern Whig*, the Belfast newspaper which spoke for Ulster liberalism, advocating catholic emancipation, non-denominational education, parliamentary reform, the abolition of slavery, the repeal of the corn laws, denouncing the evils of Irish landlordism and of the established church, but supporting the union with Britain. Finlay's devotion to liberalism is reflected in the names he bestowed on his sons – George Washington, Henry Montgomery and Hamilton Rowan.

Porter's reputation was not confined to Belfast or to Ireland; he was well known in unitarian circles in Britain as well. Many of the students he lectured to in Belfast went as ministers to congregations in Britain, as did one of his own clerical brothers, James Nixon, so that he had a widely dispersed network of acquaintances in Britain and even beyond, for at least one went to Montreal and another to Adelaide. And through the Chamberlains and their relatives the Nettlefolds and the Prestons and former pupils of his London school, he was known among English liberals.

John Scott Porter's brother William was the other member of the family in this generation to make a notable contribution to liberalism. Since higher education was affordable at the time for the elder son only, William was apprenticed to John Classen, a prosperous iron and timber merchant in Dublin, the brother of Revd William Porter's second wife. The Classens belonged to the Strand Road presbyterian church in Dublin, a New Light congregation. William Porter proved to have no aptitude for business; his interests were literary and historical and he showed talent as a public speaker so the Classens suggested that he should turn to law and John Classen undertook to support him financially until, in 1831, he was called to the bar. During the eight years he practised on the north-east circuit Porter took no part in politics, but his closest associates at the bar were leading liberals and like some of them he was a beneficiary of O'Connell's understanding with the whigs when he was appointed attorney general of the Cape Colony in 1839.

William Porter was only the second attorney general of the colony, for the Cape did not become a permanent part of the empire till 1814 and was still in the process of being fully integrated. Porter's post was primarily a legal one but as legal adviser to the governor and a member of both the executive and legislative councils he was involved in political issues as well. The nature of his office and the evolutionary state of the colony enabled him to influence developments; his professional ability and personal magnetism won him respect in the colony; and the confidence placed in him by the Colonial Office in London resulted in his becoming the most influential public figure of his day in the Cape Colony.

As a legal officer in a racially-divided colony Porter strove for absolute equality before the law for all, regardless of class or race. The same principle of equality of treatment was basic to the constitution he drafted when responsible government was established in the colony. Believing that justice and expediency required the inclusion of black men, he fixed a low property qualification and gave the vote to all men, regardless of race, thereby, as he said, excluding nothing but vagrancy and crime. As an *ex-officio* member of the new parliament and after his retirement from the attorney generalship in 1865 as an elected member of the house of assembly he contributed greatly to the smooth working of parliament. When the imperial government decided to extend responsible government to the Cape the governor called upon Porter to draw up the constitutional amendment. When it was passed the governor pressed Porter to become the first prime minister. He declined, as he had done offers of promotion and honours in the past – elevation to the bench, a knighthood, his portrait in oils; when the Cape parliament voted him full salary on his retirement instead of the normal pension he directed that the difference between the two should be paid to the board of examiners, the forerunner of the University of the Cape of Good Hope. In 1873, after thirty-four years in the colony, he returned to Belfast and lived for the last seven years of his life with his brother John Scott. The two died within a week of one another in July 1880.

A year later, a third generation member of the family came to prominence in liberal circles. This was Andrew Marshall Porter, John Scott's eldest son. After graduating at the Queen's College in Belfast he was called to the Irish bar in 1860. He practised on the north east circuit, took silk in 1872 and became a bencher of the King's Inn in 1878. In November 1881 he was appointed solicitor general and the following month he was elected as MP for County Londonderry in succession to Hugh Law, Q.C., who had been appointed lord chancellor of Ireland. Porter was one of the last liberal candidates to benefit from the popularity of Gladstone's reforms with the Ulster electorate before the political and constitutional changes of the 1880s swept the Ulster liberals out of existence as a party.

As a member of parliament Porter was accepted by his colleagues as a useful acquisition and was noticed by Gladstone himself. Joseph Chamberlain greeted him with the assertion that the last time they had met was when they had been playing as children in the garden at the Chamberlain home in Highbury Place and had blown up a snail with gunpowder. It was a time of high tension in Ireland. The Land League was still waging war on landlordism; Parnell and his principal henchmen were in jail, the tenant farmers were beginning to try out the land act of 1881. In May 1882 a new conciliatory policy was put into operation. Parnell and the others were released, the hard-line chief secretary W. E. Forster resigned and a new lord lieutenant, Earl Spencer, and a new chief secretary, Lord Frederick Cavendish, were appointed. On the very day of his arrival Lord Frederick and Thomas Henry Burke, the undersecretary, were assassinated when they were walking home to their official residencies in the Phoenix Park. This sensational development had unexpected repercussions for Porter; Gladstone offered him the Irish chief secretaryship in succession to the murdered Cavendish. Porter declined the offer, pleading family reasons, but the fact was he was a lawyer by inclination, not a politician and he was only in politics as a recognised path to judicial office. He was not, however, to escape involvement in the aftermath of the Phoenix Park murders; in January 1883 he was appointed Attorney General, so it fell to his lot to lead the prosecution of the band of Invincibles who were rounded up and put on trial a month later. It was a trial made memorable by the apostasy of the chief conspirator, James Carey, who turned informer, thereby ensuring the hanging of five of his companions, and by his own subsequent murder on board ship off the South African coast on his way to a safe haven in the colony of Natal.

Carey's murderer was hanged in December 1883 and in the same month Porter was raised to the bench as Master of the Rolls, an office he held for an unprecedented twenty-three years. He was created a baronet in 1902. He died in 1919, the year before the union of Great Britain and Ireland came to an end with the passing of the Government of Ireland Act in 1920.

Select bibliography

J. Bardon, *History of Ulster*, Belfast, 1992.
J.L. Garvin, *Life of Joseph Chamberlain*, 1, London, 1932.
J.L. McCracken, *New Light at the Cape of Good Hope: William Porter: The father of Cape liberalism*, Belfast, 1993.
Memorial addresses and sermons occasioned by the death of Rev John Scott Porter and Hon. William Porter, Belfast, 1880.
B.M. Walker, *Ulster politics, the formative years, 1868-86*, Belfast, 1989.
F. Wright, *Two lands on one soil*, Dublin, 1996.

DRAWING BLOOD FROM THE STONES: THE GIANT'S CAUSEWAY CASE OF 1897*

Ian Montgomery

The Giant's Causeway is a world-famous tourist venue spectacularly situated on the precipitous coastal cliffs of North Antrim, some two miles north of the town of Bushmills. This remarkable geological phenomenon has long been regarded as one of the Natural Wonders of the World on account of the spectacular and many-sided columns of rock that formed thousands of years ago from the cooling volcanic basalt. It has consistently been the most popular visitor attraction in Northern Ireland. One of the more memorable cases to come before the Irish Court of Chancellery during the nineteenth century concerned the right of the public to visit the Giant's Causeway.

Among the interested parties was the 11th Earl of Antrim, whose family papers, along with other papers bearing on the case, are available for consultation in PRONI. The legal proceedings involved a commercial syndicate, which intended to fence off the Causeway and charge for admission, and three public–spirited citizens representing the Giant's Causeway Defence Committee which had been formed to protect the public's right of access to the site. Although not formally a party to the proceedings, the Earl of Antrim was also represented at the trial as his family had long claimed to be the rightful owners of the Causeway. As well as addressing an important issue in Irish property law, this trial brought to a head a dispute that had simmered for most of the nineteenth century.[1]

Going to see the Causeway

The first known accounts of a trip to see the Giant's Causeway can be found in the descriptions, written by members of the Dublin Philosophical Society, which appeared in the *Philosophical Transactions of the Royal Society of London* between 1693 and 1698.[2] These articles, and the accompanying engravings, introduced the Causeway to the world both as a natural wonder and as an object of scientific curiosity. The reputation of the Causeway was further enhanced in the eighteenth century by the widespread dissemination of a pair of engravings by the London engraver François Vivarès, based on water colours by an otherwise obscure Dublin artist, Susanna Drury.[3] These pictures, the result of daily visits to the Causeway by the artist over a period of three months in 1740, were by far the most accurate representations of the area to have appeared. They helped to reawaken scientific interest in the Causeway and the ensuing debate on the origins of basalt, between the 'Neptunists' or 'Watermen' and the 'Vulcanists' or 'Firemen', was central to the development of geological theory in eighteenth-century Europe.[4] The reputation of the Causeway grew across Europe and, despite its relatively remote location, an increasing number of travellers came to see this wonder for themselves.

Early visitors to the Causeway found the journey difficult and accommodation scarce but as the number of tourists increased improvements were made. Towards the end of the eighteenth century the so-called 'Quality Road' was constructed from the cliff tops down to the shore, allegedly at the instigation of Frederick Hervey, the famous Earl Bishop of Derry. During the nineteenth century the whole of the north Antrim coast was made much more accessible, first by the construction of the Antrim coast road between 1832 and 1842 and then by the arrival of the railway. The line from Belfast to Ballymena was extended to Portrush in 1855 and in 1880 a branch line from Ballymoney to Ballycastle was opened. In addition to the road and rail links, there were regular steam ship services to Portrush and Ballycastle during the summer months. In 1883, an electric tramway was constructed from Portrush to Bushmills and this was extended to the Causeway in 1887.[5] The Causeway coast was now within the reach of a much greater number of visitors, including day-trippers from the industrial towns of the north of Ireland. By the end of the nineteenth century, middle- and working-class families could afford seaside holidays and a trip to the Causeway was a popular attraction – one estimate put the number of visitors to the Causeway at around 80,000 a year by the end of the century.[6]

As a result of this influx of people, the Giant's Causeway became commercialised. There was an inn near the Causeway from 1831 (which later became the Causeway Hotel) and a second, Kane's (later the Royal Hotel), was built in 1863. Local people serviced the crowds of visitors, finding employment as guides, boatmen or souvenir sellers. It is not surprising, therefore, that Hugh Lecky, the owner of the land around the Causeway, sought to obtain some financial benefit from this popular attraction. The Giant's Causeway Company, formed in 1896 and composed mainly of Lecky's relatives, leased the land between the cliff tops and the shore that included the Causeway from Hugh Lecky. According to the Articles of Association, the object of the Company was:

> To protect the Giant's Causeway from injury by trespassers, afford increased facilities for the enjoyment thereof by tourists and others and make regulations as to the charge, tolls and fees for admission thereto... [7]

In practice, this meant fencing off the Causeway and charging visitors six pence a head. The idea of admission charges produced a storm of protest locally and nationally and the Giant's Causeway Defence Committee was formed to mount a legal challenge to the Company. The Syndicate's plans were also opposed by William Randal MacDonnell, the 11th Earl of Antrim, who claimed ownership of the Causeway in his capacity as the 'Lord of the Soil'.

The Earls of Antrim and the Causeway

The MacDonnells had established themselves in County Antrim during the fourteenth century. They were originally a branch of Clan Donald, the great Scottish family who, as Lords of the Isles, had controlled a territory that at one time embraced most of the western seaboard of Scotland. The MacDonnells of Clan Ian Mór made themselves Lords of the Glynns and by the end of the sixteenth century they had ousted the MacQuillans from the neighbouring Lordship of the Route. Unlike most of the other Gaelic families in Ulster, they survived the era of plantation and confiscation. James VI & I created Randal 'Arranach' MacDonnell, Viscount Dunluce and Earl of Antrim and granted him a charter that recognised his ownership of the four northern baronies of County Antrim, an area of some 330,000 acres (approximately 520 square miles). Subsequent Earls of Antrim were unable to retain control of all of this vast estate but they remained substantial landowners in County Antrim until the end of the nineteenth century.[8]

The earliest reference to the Causeway in the Antrim Estate Papers occurs in a survey of the estate made in 1734. Interestingly, although the surveyor was a local man, the Causeway is shown on the survey map in the townland of Ardihanan rather than in the neighbouring townland of Ardsoughteragh (modern Aird) where it is in fact located. At the time of the survey, Aird was leased to a John McCollum who, in 1738, converted this lease into a fee-farm grant, a permanent lease at a small fixed rent. This fee-farm grant effectively alienated the property from the Antrim Estate. The land passed by marriage into the hands of another local land-owning family, the Leckys of Beardiville, in 1796.[9]

During the early part of the nineteenth century, a number of legal disputes occurred concerning the ownership of the Causeway. The Antrim family claimed that the lands granted in the original fee-farm deed extended only to the edge of the cliffs above the Causeway. They also claimed mineral rights over the whole area as the rights to quarries and minerals had been specifically reserved to the Earls of Antrim in the deed. Special provision had been made for the Causeway and Dunluce Castle, the historic stronghold of the Antrim MacDonnells, in the various settlements of the Antrim Estate that were made during the early nineteenth century. This suggests that ownership of the Causeway retained at least symbolic importance for the family and they appear to have regarded themselves as the guardians of the site. In 1825, after the captain of a Royal Navy ship had removed some stones from the Causeway, Lord Mark Kerr[10] complained to the Admiralty on behalf of the family. Not only did he assert the family's proprietorial rights to the Causeway, but he demanded that the Admiralty take steps to prevent any recurrence of this vandalism, as:

> ... this Causeway is considered not only one of the greatest wonders in Great Briton [*sic*] but throughout all Europe and the preservation of it a matter of general consequence to the whole world.[11]

The Leckys never accepted the alleged rights of the Antrim Estate over the Causeway. In 1826 and 1833 the Antrim family publicised their claims to the Causeway by erecting pillars near the Giant's Well. When Hugh Lecky had them removed – to defend the 'right of property' – legal action was threatened but did not materialise. The issue arose again in the 1840s when, on Lecky's orders, columns were removed from the main Causeway for building work and again in 1863 when he had a house built on the edge of the Causeway. This was a substantial two-storey house, which necessitated the levelling of part of the Causeway. In this latter case, Lord Antrim's solicitors objected not only on legal grounds but also on what they described as public grounds, as they claimed that the building:

> ... offends the public taste, and is generally considered to mar the beauty of the Causeway and the surrounding scenery...

Again, the issue of ownership of the Causeway was not resolved, probably because the Antrim Estate was reluctant to incur the costs of court action.[12]

One way that the Antrim Estate asserted its claims to the Causeway was by appointing caretakers. Neal McMullen was employed from the 1820s until at least the 1840s 'for watching and looking to it' and in the 1860s and 1870s the caretaker was Alex Laverty.[13] It is clear from Laverty's surviving correspondence that trying to maintain some sort of control over the Causeway was a difficult and somewhat thankless task and that his relations with the Causeway guides were often strained. In 1868, for instance, he came across one of the guides, John McLaughlin, expansively informing a party of American visitors that they could pick any pillar they liked from the Causeway and have it shipped home via Liverpool. Laverty intervened at this point only to be meet with a torrent of abuse from McLaughlin and the thwarted souvenir hunters.[14]

The practice of removing stones from the Causeway had a long history. No sooner had the scientific community discovered the Causeway in the seventeenth century than they began removing pieces for further study. Less serious visitors took everything from small pieces of stone to entire columns. In response to newspaper reports that shiploads of stones were being removed from the Causeway in the 1870s, Lord Antrim's agent conducted an investigation into the practice. He concluded that no stones were being removed from the Causeway at that time but that a number of local quarries, principally those at Glenstaghy and Lemanagh near Ballintoy, produced identical stone, which was being sold as Causeway souvenirs.[15] Many visitors continued to make their own arrangements however, in spite of Laverty's best efforts, although on one occasion he managed to force an erring visitor to accompany him to Bushmills Police Station and the Earl received a written apology from the chastened souvenir hunter. Local people also had to be watched, as they tried to remove stones for building. Significantly, in the light of later events, there is no record of the Antrim Estate attempting to prosecute anyone for offences against the Causeway.[16]

The Earl of Antrim claimed the right to any timber or other goods washed up on the Causeway and Laverty was kept busy claiming this material. In these cases, he also had to watch local landowners such as the Macnaghtens who attempted to grab anything valuable found near their land.[17] Laverty's correspondence also shows that Sir Edmund Macnaghten was extracting lignite from the cliff faces above the Causeway in the 1870s.[18] When Alex Laverty died in 1877 he was not replaced as caretaker, although his widow continued to report problems at the Causeway, such as local people spreading seaweed to dry on the stones, thus making progress difficult for the tourists.[19]

The Antrim Estate does not appear to have made any further attempt to assert its rights to the Causeway until 1896 when the Giant's Causeway Company was formed. The head of the family at this time was the 11th Earl, a formidable and somewhat eccentric figure, known to his family as 'the buzzard'. Although best remembered for his often violent temper and his delight in embarrassing his more conventional relatives, he was also an efficient and shrewd manager of the family property. The Antrim Estate, already loaded down with debt by improvident owners in the seventeenth and eighteenth centuries, was the subject of a prolonged legal battle at the beginning of the nineteenth century. The eventual division of the Estate, and the associated legal costs, reduced the Earl of Antrim's holding to about 34,000 acres. The 11th Earl worked hard to clear the estate of debts and encumbrances as well as attempting to reassert his residual rights over alienated lands. The short-lived mining boom in northern and central Antrim in the later part of the nineteenth century benefited the Estate as the Earls of Antrim claimed royalties on minerals extracted. The claim to mineral rights over the Causeway was more than a technicality; the Antrim Estate had an interest in asserting such rights whenever it could.[20]

The Earl had gained a reputation for fiercely pursuing litigation. His most celebrated previous case had been against his local Rector, the Revd Dudly-Janns. This gentleman claimed that a road from his rectory to Glenarm church, which passed through the Antrim demesne, was a public highway. In this case, it was Lord Antrim who successfully defended the 'rights of property'. Not content with his victory, the Earl enthusiastically pursued a lifelong feud with the unfortunate Rector. As well as bricking-up the Antrim family's private entrance to Glenarm church, he thereafter kept his eyes firmly closed whenever he encountered Dudly-Janns to emphasise that he 'couldn't stand the sight of the fellow'. The Earl was not a man who would normally allow any infringement on his rights, or supposed rights, to pass unchallenged.[21]

The Causeway Defence Committee

Most of those who opposed the plans of the Giant's Causeway Company were not concerned with questions of ownership or proprietary rights but with public access. Many local people feared that the imposition of an entry charge to the Causeway would damage the tourist industry along the whole of the north Antrim coast. The Traill family, major shareholders in the Giant's Causeway Tramway and the Causeway Hotel, were amongst the most prominent local opponents. Local authorities in Counties Antrim and Londonderry passed resolutions protesting at what one councillor called 'a crying-out evil'.[22] Opposition to the proposals soon spread well beyond the Antrim coast and was based on the belief that the public had a long established right of entry on to the Causeway. As a Belfast newspaper put it:

> ... the public of the north of Ireland, who are naturally proud of their Causeway refused to believe that this most marvellous piece of great nature's handiwork could be treated like ordinary property, or converted from a natural temple to a proprietary peepshow.[23]

Some of the opposition to the Causeway Company took on a political complexion and a number of prominent 'Tenant Right' campaigners joined the protests against what they claimed was an arbitrary exaction by a rapacious landlord. 'The scenery of Ireland is the nation's property' thundered one Dublin paper, predicting that the Causeway proposals would be the first of many attempts to 'lay unholy hands on all the beauty spots of our land.'[24]

Opposition also came from members of the Belfast commercial and professional classes, particularly those with antiquarian and scientific interests. A Causeway Defence Committee was formed in Belfast chaired by the Lord Mayor, Sir William Pirrie, and included a number of prominent industrialists and political figures. They began to raise funds to support legal action against the Syndicate. The campaign also spread beyond Ireland. Questions were asked in Parliament, but the government refused to be drawn into the dispute. The Commons Preservation Society and the National Footpath Preservation Society in London also became involved, testimony to the growing interest in the question of access to the countryside in late Victorian Britain.[25]

One of the Causeway Company's first acts was to appoint William Taylor, just retired as police sergeant in Bushmills, as caretaker of the Causeway. They also began preparations for the erection of a fence around the site. Metal railings were manufactured and transported to the vicinity – with some difficulty as the Causeway Tramway refused to carry them. The hostility generated by the anti-enclosure campaign made the Syndicate hesitate before erecting the fence. Several newspaper articles had alluded to an incident in London a few years previously when railings erected around Hyde Park had been torn down by an angry mob. Although holes had been bored in the rock to support the fencing, it was reported that part of the large crowd of people who had visited the Causeway on the 13 July holiday had filled them in again.[26] A number of prominent opponents of the enclosure made a point of walking over the Causeway without payment and it was evident that court action would be necessary before the Company could proceed to collect gate money. Accordingly, the company took an action in the Chancery Court against three prominent members of the Defence Committee, seeking an injunction preventing them from trespassing on the Causeway. In order to make any judgement binding on the public at large, an injunction was also sought against the Attorney General of Ireland.

There was probably some measure of collusion between the Company and the Defence Committee in the selection of the defendants, who were not only public figures, but also representative of the various interests opposed to the enclosure of the Causeway. Lavens Ewart, a director of the linen manufacturers, William Ewart & Sons, and a Belfast Alderman, was a younger son of the industrialist and Conservative MP Sir William Ewart. Robert Young was a prominent Belfast architect with antiquarian interests and the author of several works on local history. The third defendant, Samuel McElroy, was a veteran tenant right campaigner who had stood, unsuccessfully, for parliament in North Antrim as a Gladstonian Liberal. He was also editor of the *Ballymoney Free Press*. In the opinion of a local newspaper they represented respectively:

> ... the manufacturing and commercial classes, ... the literary and professional classes, [and] ... the agricultural classes and local people generally.[27]

In the event, Lord Antrim was not a party to the proceedings, although he retained a barrister to watch the case on his behalf. The Defence Committee attempted to persuade him to pursue his legal claims to the Causeway but he decided that the estate had little to gain from an expensive legal challenge to the Lecky family. However, his agent supplied the defence with copies of documents from the Estate papers.[28]

While the defendants refused to acknowledge the Lecky family's ownership of the Causeway, the main claim they made was that a public right of way existed from the Causeway Head across the foreshore to the Grand Causeway and other 'points of interest'. They also claimed that there was a customary right of access to the Causeway from time immemorial. The Attorney General, on behalf of the general public, supported the claim that:

> ... from the time whereof the memory of man is not to the contrary, [there] hath been a certain ancient and laudable custom there used and approved of that the persons inhabiting the said district have had, and have used, and have been accustomed, and of right ought to have had, and still of right ought to have full and free liberty and privilege of entering into and upon the said premises known as the Giant's Causeway ... and of examining and viewing the formation of the said Giant's Causeway, and for walking and exercising themselves thereon, and of pic-nicing, and otherwise enjoying themselves on the said Causeway in any lawful and innocent recreation at any time of year.[29]

The case comes to court

The case was heard before Vice-Chancellor Chatterton in Dublin in March 1897 and lasted for seven days. No less than nine barristers were engaged, those for the defendants being led by the colourful Hugh Macdermot QC. Known as The Macdermot, the hereditary 'Prince of Coolavin' had been Attorney General of Ireland in Gladstone's administration a few years previously. Much excitement had been generated in the press during the run up to the trial with a great deal of hostile criticism aimed at the members of the Causeway Company. During the second day of the trial, the Company's counsel complained to the Vice-Chancellor about an advertisement that had appeared in a Dublin newspaper for a poem called *The Giant in his Causeway*, by the Revd Thomas Mills. The poem accused those involved in the Causeway Syndicate of being, *inter alia:*

Poor pigmies of a low, degenerate birth,
Unborn of heaven, and sprung alone from earth,
How far removed from our primordial races,
Who hold their home as heaven's free open spaces?

The judge, while holding that it was both a contemptible poem and probably a contempt of court, decided not to take any action against the paper.[30]

A total of 32 witnesses were called during the course of the trial. Some of them were professional men such as surveyors and photographers, but most were ordinary people who lived and worked around the Causeway. The evidence of these people, the guides, boatmen and tenant farmers, was necessary in order to establish who, if anyone, had controlled the Causeway on a day-to-day basis. The Causeway Company opened the case and sought to demonstrate that the Lecky family had exercised effective control over the Causeway for as long as anyone could remember. They were able to show that the area between the cliff tops and the shore had been grazed, mainly by sheep, but also by horses and cattle, over the previous 60 years. There was much discussion concerning how far over the main Causeway the grass extended, as this was important in establishing whether the Grand Causeway itself could be considered to be part of Lecky's grazing land. Evidence was also given about the gathering of seaweed and kelp-burning on the Causeway shore.[31]

The Company's counsel also made much of various 'acts of ownership' which the Lecky family had performed on the Causeway. These included creating a path along the cliff tops to Plaiskin Head for the visit to the Causeway of the British Association for the Advancement of Science in 1874, and cutting a path through 'The Loom', close to the Causeway itself, in 1852. The building of the Causeway House in 1863 was described in some detail, as it was the most emphatic of Lecky's acts of ownership. This last act invoked a particularly indignant response from The Macdermot, who claimed that the house had been erected with the sole purpose of annoying Lord Antrim. Noting that Mrs Lecky had laid the foundation stone, he declared that:

> It certainly needed the grace of Mrs Lecky's presence to palliate to some extent the bad taste shown in the erection of this miserable lodge, devoid of any quality of grace or beauty.[32]

By the time the trial began the Causeway House was occupied by Sergeant Taylor, the Causeway Company's caretaker. Before this, the occupants had been tenants of the Lecky family who were paid small sums to look after the Giant's Well. Various witnesses were able to recite the names of those who had supplied visitors with water (and occasionally whiskey) at the Giant's Well. The earliest mentioned were Lilly McMullen and Anne Campbell, either of whom could have been the 'old grey hag' described by William Thackeray in *The Irish Sketchbook*, who sold good whiskey but had never been known to have change for a shilling.[33] Margaret McKinley, who gave evidence at the hearing, had occupied the Causeway House immediately before Taylor. She gave her age under oath as 'about thirty', although an unkind journalist estimated it as closer to eighty, and her memory of the Causeway stretched back at least forty years. Mrs McKinley was rather coy about the availability of whiskey as well as water at the Giant's Well, much to the disappointment of the Macdermot. The defence was sceptical of the claim that the people at the well were caretakers of the Causeway and no evidence was offered that Lecky's nominees had exercised any supervision over the Causeway.

The Causeway guides

Among the most interesting witnesses to be called were the Causeway guides. There appear to have been guides at the Causeway for nearly as long as there were visitors. As early as 1708, Thomas Molyneux had hired a guide at Ballymoney to show him to the Causeway.[34] By the middle of the eighteenth century, the guides were an established feature. When Mary Delany and her friends had their picnic on the Causeway in 1758, they were surrounded by an entourage that included, along with their own servants:

> ... women and children that gathered seaweed and shells for us, about twelve in number, ... on the right hand men that were our guides, of different ages seated on points of rocks, whose figures were very droll...[35]

Later commentators failed to find the guides so amusing. In 1811 the poet and geologist William Drummond likened these 'courteous sans culottes' to flies and added:

> The guides do not exhibit the character of the Irish peasantry in the most favourable light. They are envious, litigious, and corrupted by idleness, and their dependence on the precarious bounty of strangers.[36]

The writers of the Ordnance Survey Memoirs expressed similar sentiments in the 1830s. While they found most of the inhabitants of the Parish of Billy to be industrious, this was not the case on the sea coast:

> ... where idleness prevails to a great extent owing to the nature of their usual occupation which, though sometimes very profitable, is nonetheless very precarious, viz., acting as guides to the great variety of strangers visiting the great national curiosity. ... On the approach ... of a set of visitors, they generally quit their occupations, even though they may be successful ones, to surround the strangers, upon whom they often force their services as guides.[37]

This observation bears out the celebrated account in Thackeray's *Irish Sketchbook* of the hapless traveller being bundled into a boat by a group of guides and kept tossing up and down on the swell until he had bought an appropriate number of geological 'samples'.[38] The guides did have some defenders however. Members of the Belfast Naturalists' Field Club, writing in 1874, declared that the guides were '...really necessary and often hard-working attendants' and pointed out that the geological samples or specimens had to be collected at some risk to life and limb during the winter months.[39]

Most of the guides called as witnesses at the trial were elderly. Alexander McMullen, an occasional guide, was 76 and had started selling boxes of 'specimens' to tourists at the age of 15. Both his father and grandfather had been guides before him, a family tradition that stretched back into the eighteenth century. He had also worked as a boatman, taking groups and visitors around the nearby caves and in good weather landing them near The Keystone on the east side of the Grand Causeway. By the end of the nineteenth century there were a dozen boats based at Portnaboe just below the two hotels. Most of the boatmen worked in association with one of the hotels, passing over half the fares they received to the hotel owners.

Guiding was not a full time occupation. Most, like the 82-year-old James MacAllister, fisherman, boatman and guide, had been 'about many a business'. MacAllister was rather vague about ages and dates. He had been a guide 'whilst purty young and whilst old' but declined to be more specific about ages – 'we don't keep account'. While many commentators spoke of 'hosts' of guides infesting the Causeway, 87-year-old Lydia McNaull, whose husband had taken over the Causeway Hotel in 1843 – the year after Thackeray's visit – remembered only about half a dozen when she first arrived. The number probably increased with the number of visitors – one guide reckoned numbers had increased twenty-fold over the previous fifty years. Many of the guides kept books, which were signed by distinguished visitors. David McConaghy, guide and boatman for 50 years, produced testimonials from Prince Arthur (a younger son of Queen Victoria) and the statesman Sir Stafford Northcote.

The case for the defendants

The defendants in the case sought to prove not only that the public had visited the Causeway without any objections from the owners from the end of the seventeenth century but also that public paths existed, running from the Causeway Head along the foreshore to the Grand Causeway and to other places of interest. As well as the guides and boatmen, a number of more distinguished witnesses were called to testify on these matters. Both sides produced sets of photographs to illustrate their case. The defendants' were taken by Robert Welch, the leading commercial photographer in the north of Ireland. Welch, a member of the Belfast Naturalists' Field Club like many of those involved in the case, testified that he had been taking photographs of the Causeway for fourteen years. His photographs of the Causeway and the surrounding area are still highly regarded and continue to feature in geological textbooks.[40]

The most prominent local resident to be called was Dr Anthony Traill, Fellow, and later Provost, of Trinity College, Dublin. With his brother William, he had developed the Causeway Tramway and William Traill also owned the Causeway Hotel. Dr Traill cheerfully admitted to a vested interest in preserving free access to the Causeway. The Tramway had run at a loss during its early years, but in 1896 some 100,000 passengers had been carried and around 150,000 were expected the next year. This success was threatened if the Causeway became a less attractive destination for visitors. Traill had been born less than three miles from the Causeway and he still lived in the area. Like other local witnesses, he gave evidence concerning the large number of visitors who frequented the place. He had done the honours for 'all the swells of every kind' including Lord Zetland, a former Viceroy of Ireland. Prince Edward of Saxe-Weimar, a cousin of Queen Victoria and Commander in Chief of the army in Ireland, had also seen part of the

Causeway, but Traill thought him too heavy to risk on some of the paths.

Another witness who was well acquainted with the Causeway was the formidable senior Presbyterian minister in Portrush Jonathan Simpson, who described himself as an 'honorary guide'. Now 81, he entertained the court with his memories of the Causeway stretching back over 70 years, which included walking from the Causeway to Carrickareade and back at the age of 10 to 'handsel' (i.e. break-in) his first jacket and pants. He had conducted a large number of parties over the Causeway, on one occasion escorting 230 Presbyterian ministers and their wives along the precipitous Shepherd's Path. This evidence was the excuse for some unfortunate puns on the subject of pastors and shepherds from The Macdermot. Two of the defendants, Ewart and McElroy, also gave evidence to explain the rights over the Causeway that they claimed. McElroy's performance in the witness box probably did more harm than good to the defendants' case, as he could not resist the temptation to make speeches, rather than answer questions.

In order to establish the antiquity of their claims to free public access to the Causeway, the defence produced a number of items of historical interest. They located a Grand Jury presentment from 1814 that showed that the road along the foreshore, from the Stookans to the Causeway, had been repaired at public expense. The road was described as running from Dervock to the sea and the defendants claimed that this proved that the road that led to the Causeway was a public highway. The Macdermot next produced the original Ordnance Survey map of the area dating from 1832 which, he claimed, showed public roads crossing the Causeway. After lengthy legal argument this map was admitted as evidence, the first time an Ordnance Survey map had ever been accepted as an exhibit in a case of this kind. Two other items produced by the defence did not fare so well. The Secretary of the Royal Dublin Society produced two engravings that usually hung on the walls of Leinster House. These were Edwin Sandys' prospect of the Causeway, made in 1696 and later published in the *Transactions* of the Royal Society in London, and the celebrated Vivarès engravings of Susan Drury's watercolours, which were published in 1743. The Sandys picture was of particular interest to the defence as it showed a distinct path winding across the foreshore to the main Causeway. The Syndicate's lawyers challenged the accuracy and provenance of both engravings – the case for the Sandys drawing was not helped by the fact that he had placed the Causeway north-west of Coleraine rather than north-east. After lengthy legal arguments, the judge refused to admit the engravings as evidence.[41]

There were clear signs that by the end of the trial the Vice-Chancellor was getting rather bored with the repetitive nature of much of the evidence. When one of the last witnesses, Seaton Milligan – another Belfast industrialist – appeared, he got rather short shrift. In spite of reciting an impressive list of scholarly credentials: Honorary Secretary of the Ulster Antiquarian Society, Vice-president of the Royal Society of Antiquaries of Ireland, member of the Royal Irish Academy, etc., he found the judge unwilling to listen to his speculations on the origins of the Causeway Fair. Several witnesses had already testified about the fair, which had been held each year, starting on the 13 August, at the top of the cliffs on the site later occupied by the Causeway Hotel. It lasted for two days, sometimes longer, and attracted visitors from a wide area who had taken the opportunity to visit the Causeway. None of this was disputed however nor, in the judge's opinion, was it very relevant.

When the Vice-Chancellor finally made his decision, he found for the plaintiffs on all points. The Lecky family's claims to ownership of the Causeway were upheld, public access to the area had only occurred with the implied consent of the owners, and the existence of public paths across the Causeway was denied. The legal arguments were repeated in the Court of Appeal at the end of 1897, but the original judgement was upheld. The Giant's Causeway Company was therefore free to erect fences and charge for admission.

The National Trust and the Causeway

In his judgement, the Vice-Chancellor stated that he:

> ... should regret if the result of my decision were to exclude visitors from a place so celebrated and so interesting as this. But I think it will probably tend in the opposite direction, for it will facilitate access to the place and improve the approaches and means of viewing it...[42]

The Vice-Chancellor's confidence was not misplaced. The Causeway Company did indeed improve access to the Causeway and visitors continued to come in great numbers. The Company also protected the

Causeway from souvenir hunters and the threat of commercial quarrying.

By the end of the Second World War, however, it was clear that the Causeway had declined in popularity as a visitor attraction. The Causeway Company's turnstile receipts show approximately 33,000 paying visitors in 1945. Although this number had risen to over 40,000 in the 1950s it was still less than half the number of visitors attracted at the beginning of the century.[43] When the Giant's Causeway Tramway closed down at the end of 1949, access to the Causeway was mainly obtained by motorcar or bus and it was clear that the approach roads needed to be upgraded. The local authorities, however, were unwilling to provide roads at public expense to a private facility. Concern was also being expressed about the rather shabby appearance of the buildings that had grown up around the Causeway and the dangerous state of some of the paths.[44]

During the appeal hearing one of the judges had noted that some of the witnesses appeared to regard the Causeway as 'a kind of national property'. There was, however, no legal means in the nineteenth century to protect such property.[45] At the height of the public controversy in 1896, one of the defendants, Samuel McElroy, suggested that the British government should follow the example of the United States and establish National Parks, with the Giant's Causeway as the first.[46] This idea was too radical for a Victorian government and Britain had to wait over fifty years for its first National Park. The idea of bringing the Causeway into public ownership was, however, revived in the 1950s when Antrim County Council considered acquiring the site. Nothing came of this proposal, but at the end of the decade the National Trust began moves to acquire the Causeway.[47]

Once again, an Earl of Antrim was involved with the fate of the Causeway. Randal, 13th Earl of Antrim, grandson of the eccentric 'Buzzard', was chairman of the Northern Ireland region of the National Trust from 1948 until 1965, and from then until 1977 national chairman. Unlike his grandfather, he was renowned for his tact and negotiating skill and he oversaw the reorganisation and expansion of the National Trust's activities. While the acquisition of the Giant's Causeway was compatible with the Trust's policy of protecting important coastal areas, a significant capital outlay was necessary to secure the site. This was provided, in part, by the Northern Ireland government which granted

£75,000 from the Ulster Land Fund, with Lord Antrim playing an important role in negotiations with the then Minister of Finance, Captain Terence O'Neill. In 1961, the National Trust purchased the interests of the company that controlled the Causeway and the freehold interest of the Lecky family and, in 1963, the Causeway was formally opened to the public free of charge.[48]

In 1960 the distinguished architect Clough Williams-Ellis visited the Causeway and advised the Trust to:

> ... purge the whole coastal territory within its care of every impertinence that could detract or distract from the appreciation of nature's great set piece. Into such high drama the petty intrusion of irrelevant little souvenir shops and kiosks is clearly improper and quite unacceptable, and clearance of all such is essential, not only to the dignity of the Causeway itself, but also to its full enjoyment by all who visit it, save, perhaps to an (at first) insensitive minority, whose winning-over to a livelier appreciation is, again, one of the Trust's objectives.[49]

This advice was followed. All the remnants of the Causeway's commercial past were removed and the new visitor facilities provided on the cliff top above the Causeway. The National Trust also acquired adjacent parts of the coast and the North Antrim Coast Path was created. The objective of the original Giant's Causeway Defence Committee, free public access, had been achieved, along with a measure of protection for the Causeway and its environment, now recognised as a World Heritage Site.[50]

NOTES

* I am grateful to a number of former colleagues in PRONI for advice and assistance in the preparation of this paper, particularly Anthony Malcomson, David Lammey, Ann McVeigh and Heather Stanley. Material held in PRONI is cited by permission of: the Deputy Keeper of the Records, Public Record Office of Northern Ireland, Viscount Dunluce; and the National Trust, Northern Ireland Region. An earlier version of this article appeared in *The Glynns*, xxvii (1999).

1 The Earl of Antrim Estate Papers (D/2977) form one of the largest collections held by PRONI. The legal papers relating to the Giant's Causeway case can be found at D/2977/2/13 and Alex Laverty's correspondence as caretaker of the Causeway at D/2977/5/2/10. The papers of the McGildowny family (D/1375), who acted as agents of the estate in the first half of the nineteenth century, are an important adjunct to the main Antrim Estate archive. The 13th Earl of Antrim's papers as Chairman of the National Trust in Northern Ireland, along with other National Trust papers, are also held in PRONI (D/3839). For the other side of the story, the papers of the Lecky family are available (D/1946 & T/1113) as are those of one of the companies which controlled the Causeway, the Giant's Causeway Reversionary Trustees (D/2241).

2 Sir Richard Bulkeley, 'Part of a letter from Sir R. B., S.R.S. to Dr Lister, concerning the Giant's Causeway in the County of Antrim [sic] in Ireland' in R. *Soc. Phil. Trans.*, no 199 (April 1693), pp. 708-11; Rev Dr Samuel Foley, 'An account of the Giant's Causeway in the north of Ireland' in R. Soc. Phil. Trans., no. 212 (July-August 1694), pp. 170-5; Thomas Molyneaux, 'Some notes upon the foregoing account of the Giant's Causeway, serving to further illustrate the same' in R. Soc. Phil. Trans., no. 212 (July-August 1694), pp. 175-82; Thomas Molyneaux, 'A letter to Dr Martin Lister containing some additional observations on the Giant's Causeway in Ireland' in R. Soc. Phil. Trans., no. 241 (May 1698), pp. 209-23. For more information about the members of the Dublin Philosophical Society and their interest in the Causeway see K. T. Hoppen, *The common scientist in the seventeenth century* (London, 1970) and idem, 'The papers of the Dublin Philosophical Society, 1683-

1708: introductory material and index' in *Ana. Hib.*, xxx (1982), pp. 151-248.

3 Martyn Anglesea & John Preston, 'A Philosophical landscape' Susanna Drury and the Giant's Causeway' in *Art History*, iii, no 5 (1980), pp. 252-73.

4 Patrick N. Wyse Jackson, 'Fluctuations in fortune: thre hundred years of Irish geology' in John Wilson Foster (ed.), *Nature in Ireland: a scientific and cultural history* (Dublin, 1997), pp 91-114.

5 For the development of the railway system in north Antrim see: J.R.L. Currie, *The Northern Counties Railway, Vol. I: beginnings and development, 1845-1903* (Newton Abbot, 1973) and J. H. McGuigan, *The Giant's Causeway Tramway* (Lingfield, Surrey, 1964). Papers relating to the Giant's Causeway, Portrush and Bush Valley Tramway and Railway Company are held by PRONI under reference numbers D/392 & D/945.

6 For accounts of the development of the Causeway's reputation and the resulting tourism see: Martyn Anglesea, 'The iconography of the Antrim coast' in Gerald Dawe & John Wilson Foster (ed.), *The poet's place: Ulster literature and society. Essays in honour of John Hewitt, 1907-87* (Belfast, 1991), pp. 31-44; Robin Fedden, *The Giant's Causeway: an illustrated account* (London, 1971); Donal P. McCraken, 'Beyond the Glynns': the phenomenon of the Giant's Causeway in Georgian Ireland' in *The Glynns*, xiii (1985), pp. 21-5; Julia E. Mullin, *The Causeway Coast* (Belfast, [1974]); Philip Watson, *The Giant's Causeway and the north Antrim coast (*Dublin, 2000).

7 Memorandum and Articles of Association of the Giant's Causeway Company Ltd. (PRONI, COM/40/1/G8).

8 The most complete history of the Earls of Antrim is George Hill, *An historical account of the MacDonnells of Antrim: including notices of some other septs, Irish and Scottish* (Belfast, 1873), see also: Ian Montgomery, 'The Earl of Antrim Estate Papers' in The Glynns, xxiv (1996), pp. 22-9.

9 'Survey of the Barony of Cary' by Archibald Stewart, 1734 (PRONI, D/2977/35/1). The Lecky family's title to Aird townland is set out in the printed *Brief on hearing of appeal*, pp. 4-6 (PRONI, D/1977/2/13/2/1).

10 When the 6th Earl of Antrim died in 1791 without leaving a legitimate male heir, the Antrim Estates were divided between his

daughters Anne Catherine, who became Countess of Antrim 'in her own right', and Charlotte, who married Lord Mark Kerr, a younger son of the Marquis of Lothian. For a full account of the division of the estate see A.P.W. Malcomson, *The pursuit of the heiress* (Belfast, 1982), p. 26-9.

11 Kerr to the Admiralty, 18 March 1828 (PRONI, D/2977/2/13/1/4).

12 See typescript copy correspondence between various representatives of the Antrim family and Hugh Lecky, 1833-63 (PRONI, D/1946/2/3). Quotation from Leman & Co., London to Hugh Lecky, 13 October 1863.

13 For McMullen see: Neal McMullen to Charles McGildowney, Esq, 3 August 1825 (PRONI, D/2977/2/13/1/4) and reference to 'Old McMullen' in --- to Hugh Lecky, 20 August 1844 (PRONI, D/2977/2/13/1/5). For Laverty see his correspondence with Alexander McDonald, the Antrim Estate agent, 1863-77 (PRONI).

14 Alex Laverty to Alexander McDonald, 15 July 1868 (PRONI, D/2977/5/2/10/6/1).

15 Alex Laverty to Alexander McDonald, 20 October 1868 (PRONI, D/2977/5//2/10/6/3); Daniel McKeag to Mr McDonald, 31 October 1868 (PRONI, D/2977/5/2/0/6/3).

16 Alex Laverty to Alexander McDonald, 13 September 1869 (PRONI, D/2977/5/2/10/7/1); Alex Laverty to Alexander McDonald, 2 February 1875 (PRONI, D/2977/5/2/10/13/1).

17 Alex Lavery to Alexander McDonald, 27 October 1874 (PRONI, D/2977/5/2/10/12/35).

18 Alex Laverty to Alexander McDonald, 13 February 1873 (PRONI, D/2977/5/2/10/11/2).

19 Martha A. Laverty to Alexander McDonald, 25 October 1877 (PRONI, D/2977/5/2/10/15/29).

20 Montgomery, 'The Earl of Antrim Estate Papers'.

21 The papers on the Dudly-Janns case are in the Antrim Estate papers (PRONI, D/2977/2/10). For the 11th Earl see Angela Antrim, *The Antrim MacDonnells* (Belfast, 1977).

22 See report in the *Northern Whig*, 7 July 1896.

23 See cutting from unidentified newspaper, 19 March 1987 (PRONI, D/2977/2/13/3/3).

24 *Irish Daily Independent* quoted in the *Northern Whig*, 7 July 1896.

25 See newspaper cuttings (PRONI, D/2977/2/13/1/19); *The National Footpath Preservation Society, Occasional Paper, No 64* (PRONI, D/2977/2/13/2/2).

26 See cutting from unidentified newspaper (PRONI, D/1946/6).

27 Quotation from scrapbook containing cuttings from unidentified newspaper, probably the *Northern Whig* (henceforth cited as 'Scrapbook'), 19 March 1897 (PRONI, D/2977/2/13/3/3/).

28 See correspondence between The Causeway Defence Committee and Lord Antrim, 1896-7 (PRONI, D/2977/2/13/1/2).

29 *Brief on hearing of appeal*, p. 9 (D/2977/2/13/2/1/). For a more detailed discussion of the legal issues involved see Norman Dawson, '*The Giant's Causeway case:* property law in Ireland 1845-1995' in Norma Dawson et al (ed.), *One hundred and fifty years of Irish law* (Belfast, 1996), pp. 239-57.

30 Scrapbook, 20 March 1897 (D/2977/13/3/3).

31 This account of the trial is based on the newspaper reports in the 'Scrapbook' (PRONI, D/2977/2/13/3/3) and the printed version of the original short-hand report in the *Brief on hearing of appeal*, (PRONI, D/2977/2/13/2/1).

32 'Scrapbook', 22 March 1897 (PRONI, D/2977/2/13/3/3).

33 W. M. Thackeray, *The Irish Sketch Book* (reprinted Dublin, 1990), p. 327.

34 Thomas Molyneux, 'Journey to the North, 7th August 1708' in Robert M. Young (ed.), *Historical notices of old Belfast and its vicinity* (Belfast, 1896), pp. 152-60.

35 Angélique Day (ed.), *Letters from Georgian Ireland: the correspondence of Mary Delany, 1731-68* (Belfast, 1991), pp. 150-2.

36 William Drummond, *The Giant's Causeway*, a poem (Belfast, 1811).

37 Angélique Day & Patrick McWilliams (ed.), *Ordnance Survey Memoirs of Ireland, Vol. 16, Parishes of County Antrim V* (Belfast, 1992), p. 38

38 Thackeray, *The Irish Sketch Book*, pp. 322-8.

39 Belfast Naturalists' Field Club, *Guide to Belfast and the adjacent counties* (Belfast, 1874), p. 312

40 For Welch see: E. Estyn & Brian S. Turner, *Ireland's Eye: the photographs of Robert John Welch* (Belfast, 1977). The photographs that Welch took for this trial do not appear to have survived.

41 These views had probably been discovered by Robert Young, one of the defendants, see: Robert M. Young, 'Early notices and

engraved views of the Giant's Causeway' in *Ulster Journal of Archaeology*, iii (1898), pp. 40-9. The Sandys engraving was published as the frontispiece of *R. Soc. Phil. Trans.*, no. 235 (December 1967). For the Vivarès engravings see Anglesea & Preston, '"A Philosophical landscape": Susanna Drury and the Giant's Causeway.'

42 *Brief on hearing of appeal* (PRONI, D/2977/2/13/2/1), p. 174

43 Table of turnstile readings, 1945-61, in the 'Minute Book, Giant's Causeway Reversionary Trustees Ltd.' (PRONI, D/2241/2).

44 See newspaper cuttings in the 'Minute Book, Giant's Causeway Reversionary Trustees Ltd.' (PRONI, D/2241/2).

45 Dawson, '*The Giant's Causeway Case*', p.254.

46 His letter, dated 6 July, appears in the *Northern Whig*, 7 July 1896.

47 See newspaper cuttings in the 'Minute Book, Giant's Causeway Reversionary Trustees Ltd.' (PRONI, D/2241/2).

48 Lyn Gallagher & Dick Rogers, *Castle, coast and cottage: the National Trust in Northern Ireland* (2nd ed., Belfast, 1986).

49 The Giant's Causeway Project, Report by Clough Williams-Ellis, August 1960 (PRONI, D/3839/B/16).

50 Watson, *The Giant's Causeway.*

Letterbook of Greg & Cunningham 1756-1757: Merchants of New York and Belfast. Edited by Thomas M. Truxes. Oxford University Press, 2001; ISBN 0 19 726219 8; £50.00.

The publication of the edited correspondence from the Letterbook of Greg & Cunningham 1756-1757, who were the most successful Irish-American trading firm of the colonial period, is testimony to the immense richness of north American archival material available for the study of eighteenth-century Ireland. The Letterbook is an American record in the sense that it is part of the collection of New York Historical Society. It also has a substantial British element because Irish and American trade were both formally bound and informally conducted within the ambit of English legislature.

The title is striking enough to draw attention – merchants of New York and Belfast – for who were the men who could straddle both societies? In the Introduction, Truxes fully describes their credentials; both were prominent among the élite of northern Irish society where they were probably the wealthiest members of that business community; they were business partners, on their own and with others, in a range of commercial and manufacturing ventures in Ireland; they were brothers-in-law within a wide but close family network which spanned involvement in the Manchester cotton trade, West Indian sugar plantations, New York and Philadelphian flax seed and general export trade and Irish exports of linen and provisions.

Thomas Greg's most important contribution to the New York-based business was his authority and influence both in the north of Ireland and the London-based merchant houses which financed the north Atlantic trade. Waddell Cunningham's contribution was as a provider of investment capital in the shipping activities and in energetic negotiation of commercial deals. The Letterbook reveals the extent and intensity of these activities, many undertaken with opportunism, within a trading economy distorted by the Seven Years' War. The correspondence also offers glimpses of other aspects of that north Atlantic trade: smuggling, servants (indentured) and slavery. Paradoxically, it is the very stylised form of this business correspondence which reveals the most about the attitudes of those involved.

It is, of course, the quality of the editorial interpretation which transforms a primary record. Truxes' authoritative Introduction provides invaluable insights not only into the New York trading patterns but also the complexity and efficacy of Belfast mercantile networks. The meticulous documentation contained in the footnotes, both to the Introduction and the Correspondence, provides the genealogist as well as the research scholar with riches of information. This is an expensive book but in terms of quality it certainly provides 'best value'.

Brenda Collins

A Victorian Schoolgirl's Diary for 1884, Clara Emily Carpenter. Ed Iain T. Adamson. Pentland Press, Bishop Auckland, 2000. pp x and 285.

This clearly written memoir, the diary of sixteen-year-old Clara Emily Carpenter, is above all a memorial to a much loved, much petted, younger sister, Katie, who died in her eleventh year. The sisters are closer than many would be today, their parents more distant: the girls share a bed, the older sister mothers the younger, even nursing her when she is gravely ill. Coming to terms with this bereavement seems to be the motivation behind the diary and after a year it peters out. It tells in detail of Katie's final days, captures the memories of a last seaside holiday that she has enjoyed, and repeatedly lists the flowers laid on her grave.

> Saturday Oct 18th Went to Nunhead to plant bulbs, 5 doz. white hyacinths.

So while the diary gives us a clear sense of a sister's grief in Victorian times, and its expression in her own failing health, there is much that must also have been part of Clara's experience that she does not choose to tell us about. It is the death of her sister, and of others she knows, that she wishes to record in detail. The diary entry before the October graveyard visit reads:

> Thursday Oct 16th Ellen left; been with us for 8½ years.

A servant who has been with the family for half of Clara's life merits no more discussion. The limits the writer chooses for herself in this diary are often frustrating. It is not that Clara's life would lack interest for a modern reader. When secondary education for women was far from general, Clara attended Mary Datchelor School in Camberwell Grove, becoming a pupil teacher, and yet we learn remarkably little of this experience. Mention is made of her father going to business, and the editor's introduction tells us he was a printer, but again such details have no place in this diary. If looking for a sense of the period and place in which Clara lived, it exists more vividly in fiction. George Gissing's novel *In the Year of Jubilee,* also set in Camberwell and in the same decade, offers this more abundantly.

A diary written for oneself may appear one of the most truthful forms of communication, but it is also about creating an acceptable self-image. While today we expect teenagers to challenge their parents' values in the search for their own, Clara is the child of her age and a dutiful daughter, whose views seem to echo those of her parents. Her value as an observer is limited by this very respectability.

> Yesterday evening we went on the pier and saw Cinderella, a dramatic entertainment. I did not like it much. I don't think I shall ever go to anything of the kind again; it does not seem nice for girls to dress up in tights like men.

Good manners are more apparent than good writing. Clara does not exhibit any great curiosity about the lives of others. Nor does the diary delve into feelings and emotions other than ones her parents would think appropriate. This presumably accounts for the diary's survival. It was handed down within a family, and reminds us how selective is the survival of evidence from the past.

The editor Iain Adamson is Clara's great-nephew, and transcribing the diary has obviously been a labour of love. Adamson gives us biographical notes on some of the family members, though occasionally some more historical background might bring the story to life. Clara mentions a German doctor.

> We, Lily, Mama and I then went on to Tarn's to order a jacket for Mama and then on to Fore Street to get some woollen garments patented by a German Dr. Papa had heard of his theory that wool is the only perfect clothing and had bought some vests. He then said he would buy me some things if I liked. So accordingly we went to get them. They are very nice but very expensive. I have two combination garments, 1 pair of stays, 2 petticoats and 6 yards of lining. It cost altogether £3. 14. 0.
>
> The German Dr. advocates everything woollen, even bedclothes. But I don't think I should like to go in for such extremes as that. Mama does not believe in it at all. We did not get home till 3 o'clock.

The German doctor would have been Dr. Jaegar, and the business he started survives as *Jaegar*, which has a store today on Royal Avenue. They still sell expensive clothes, though these days men's woollen vests can no longer be found among the elegant ladies' fashions.

Jane Williams

George Sheridan. *When Turkeys Chewed Tobacco.* Pub. by Killesher Historical Society, Co. Fermanagh, 2001. pp. 239.

To those readers who have never heard of George Sheridan I will begin with a personal anecdote which I believe encompasses the significance of his contribution to life on this island and the paradoxical nature of his life and opinions. When George took seriously ill with cancer in the autumn of 1998, I was heartbroken that we would lose him and urgently felt that he should know how much he was esteemed by the community. I felt that some official recognition of his value was imperative. However sitting down to compose a letter I didn't know whether to send it to President Mary McAleese in the Republic or to the office concerned with honours in Britain, or both. George would have appreciated and felt at home with the representatives of either jurisdiction. Events quickly overtook me and the letter was never sent. Still on my hard disk I printed it out today, not without nostalgia, because I feel that the comments I made on that occasion are relevant to this introduction.

George was reared and farmed for a good part of this life on Cuilcagh Mountain, which straddles the Fermanagh/Cavan border. His townland of Gortaree was a remote spot and many of his close friends and neighbours were those in the mountain townlands on the Cavan side of the border. George hailed from a Methodist and Church of Ireland background and he attended the Church of Ireland school and church in Blacklion, Co. Cavan in the pre-partition years. He grew up in difficult times both politically and economically. George remembered the War of Independence, the Civil War and the Economic War. Consequently he became an anti-partitionist, but above all a pacifist with a keen sense of community relations. He made a wonderful contribution to community life and was loved by all who knew him.

George Sheridan was a founder member of Killesher (Florencecourt) Historical Society and of the Border Counties History Collective, the cross–border network of local history groups who employ this reviewer. George was a seanachie with a wealth of stories, an eye for detail, a keen memory and a tremendous willingness to give to others. He was a great friend of Michael J. Murphy and was recorded many times by the Irish Folklore Commission and Department of Folklore, UCD. Likewise George told stories for the Verbal Arts Centre, Derry and was recorded by many of our national institutions. He was recorded by or contributed to the 'Placenames Project' and the Anthropology departments at Queen's University Belfast; The Ulster Folk and Transport Museum, the Concise Oxford Dictionary of Ulster English, the BBC, Fermanagh County Museum and the History Collective's 'Spark' Magazine. In the urgent weeks before his death, George's stepson David obtained his blessing to collate George's own written memories and his many recordings into a publication. Over a period of two and a half years David compiled an enormous quantity of archival material from many different sources and endeavoured to thread them into a story, which assumes a natural flow. It was an immense labour of love and the best way to honour George: now his stories will live on.

I would characterise the book as a social history – of a mountain area in west Ulster, of life on the border, farming and domestic life in the early decades of the twentieth century. George never set out to write an autobiography, but rather in his stories he aimed to illustrate a past way of life dear to him, or in the case of his folktales his wish was to entertain the listener. Listener is the operative word, for this work is written in the first person exactly as it was told. This creates an immediacy, which brings the author close to the reader, and for those who knew him it brings George back to us. Historian Brian Turner has edited the text with a fine subtlety. For those interested in dialect the transcript remains true to George's manner of speech, and contains many unusual words mostly of Irish, but also of old English and Scots derivation. The editor supplies the reader with an essential glossary and geographical, historical and biographical information.

To the social and cultural historian this work is a gem. George narrates with personal detail the effects of smuggling and the economic war (not just from the humorous viewpoint), cultural practices such as that of naming fields and nicknaming people, superstitions and their sway. It is a very articulate text imbued with George's love of literature, his philosophy and value system. While in some books of this nature the articulation of the author's values through the text might be intrusive, in this instance George's point of view has such honesty and compassion it adds another dimension to the writing.

From a researcher's viewpoint I regret that the book does not have a subject index as this makes it difficult to access the multitude of topics contained in the text. I think this is a great shame, and whilst family and friends will much appreciate the index of people, the lack of a guide to subjects is a lost opportunity in a book of this importance. Whilst the process of indexing can be time consuming, a fuller contents page giving key subheadings to the various chapters would have made the book more user-friendly.

I believe that this book will make a significant contribution to the debate on cultural identity. George Sheridan challenges the stereotypes of politics and identity dominant in Northern Ireland and adds to our body of knowledge and insight into the complexity of cultural identity on the whole island. I would advocate this text for the school curriculum syllabus of Cultural Traditions, English or History. I would also recommend it simply as a heart-warming and pleasurable read.

Anita Gallagher

The Methodists in Ireland: A Short History, by Dudley Levistone Cooney, Columba Press, Dublin 2001, pp.280 + appendix, notes etc. and 16 pp. of b&w illustrations, £10.99.

Methodism in Ireland dates from the 1740s, appearing first in Dublin among soldiers, posted to Ireland, who had recently enlisted in one of the new Methodist 'societies' then being formed in England and who were keen to maintain the spiritual life they had enjoyed in those assemblies. At that time and for many years later, the people called Methodists (originally a nickname bestowed on John Wesley and his brother Charles by their rather less 'enthusiastic' fellow students at Oxford) operated as a ginger group within the Anglican Church. Both brothers – indeed all three of the surviving sons of the Rev. Samuel Wesley and his wife Susanna – were ordained as priests of the Church of England, and remained so as long as they lived. They and their followers attended services and took the sacraments in the established church (whether in Great Britain or in Ireland) till increasing numbers of later adherents abandoned the connection.

The first Wesleyan preacher to arrive in Ireland visited the Dublin society early in 1747, to be followed a few months later by the founder of Methodism himself and his brother Charles. While John Wesley's forte was powerful preaching, occasionally from borrowed pulpits but more often in the open air, Charles's was the composition of more than 6,000 hymns, some of which were to become famous. The enthusiastic singing of these verses not only expressed and reinforced the beliefs and doctrines expounded by the 'field preachers' but also gave Methodism one of its most characteristic and enduring features.

The author of this excellent short history notes that 'Methodism has been very free of heresy trials. There is no formal statement of faith which a member or minister is required to sign at any stage'. Ministers are, however, required from time to time to affirm that they believe and preach 'our doctrines' – a formula rather less constricting than the Thirty-nine Articles or the Westminster Confession. A dyed-in-the-wool-of-the-Lamb Methodist acquaintance of mine asserts that the only essential qualification is to have a strong desire to flee from the wrath to come. Total abstinence from alcohol, a prominent feature of later Methodism, was not advocated by its founder: he had no objection to beer and wine in moderate quantities, but was strongly opposed to spirits and warned too against drinking tea – on the grounds that it was an extravagant indulgence for people who ought to be frugal in their habits. Long after Wesley frugality was not only desirable but essential in Methodist manses, as this reviewer can testify. Inevitably the righteous were suspected by the less godly of humbug in such matters. In her great novel *Middlemarch*, George Eliot remarks of one of her characters: 'Some called him a Methodist, others a hypocrite, according to the resources of their vocabulary'.

The longest section of the six into which this book is divided deals in fair detail with the following topics: the spread of Methodism in Ireland and its organisation during Wesley's time and after; the long-lasting division between Wesleyans (the main body) and Primitive Wesleyans (conservatives who wanted to remain a society within the Church of Ireland when the others separated from it) and their eventual reunion; the history of Methodism during the later 1800s and early years of the twentieth century, including the effects of the First World War and of events in Ireland leading to independence and partition (one minister in Fermanagh, shot by a sentry, died later of his wounds; while four laymen were murdered in Co. Cork); the Church under two jurisdictions; its structures; and some smaller 'Connexions' as they were called, such as the early Calvinistic body patronised by Selina, countess of Huntingdon, which sent preachers of its own to Ireland and eventually became a separate denomination.

Another section deals with 'Preachers and People'. To the uninitiated 'Circuit Life' as a chapter heading perhaps suggests something electrifying; as it happens, Wesley was enthusiastic about electricity, which he thought might cure or alleviate a whole assortment of complaints, from toothache to weakness of the legs. Chapters on education (primary schools, Methodist College in Belfast, Wesley College in Dublin, Gurteen Agricultural College in Tipperary), on social concerns (Belfast Central and North Belfast Missions, The Strangers' Friend Society in Dublin, orphanages) and on manners and morals are both wide-ranging and informative. So too is a review of the work of Irish Methodists overseas. At home in the dark days of the 1970s and 1980s, notable attempts to heal the wounds of the divided community in the north were made by Eric Gallagher and Stanley Worrall among others, while the extraordinary example of Christian forgiveness set by Gordon Wilson in Enniskillen in 1987 was universally admired if not universally followed.

Among the readers of this journal, genealogists and family historians will be familiar with the sad facts of life expectancy in past generations. The Wesleys are a good example. Samuel Wesley and his wife Susanna had nineteen children in all, of whom ten survived into adulthood. John, the fourteenth, was the third boy to be given that name, two elder brothers having died in infancy. He himself aged six nearly went the same way in 1709, when a fire started by disgruntled parishioners destroyed the rectory at Epworth.

This book complements rather than supersedes earlier works by C. H. Crookshank (1888), R. Lee Cole (1960) and Fred Jeffery (1964). Its great practical virtue is that it provides students of Irish Methodism with a convenient and up-to-date view of the historial context of their researchers. Better still, it is so attractively written that that mythical creature the general reader will find much to enjoy in it. Wide-ranging, well-balanced and well-written, it is a good piece of work.

W. A. Maguire

Ireland & Scotland: Nation, Region, Identity, edited by D. Dickson, S. Duffy, C. O. Hainle & J. C. Ross. The Centre for Irish-Scottish Studies, Trinity College Dublin, 2001. ISBN 1-871408-16-4, pp. viii + 105. IR£5/ Euro 6.25. £4.

This volume was prepared as a record of the inter-disciplinary conference held in Trinity College Dublin and the Irish Film Centre on the 29 and 30 September 2000. It is dedicated to the memory of Donald Dewar, First Minister for Scotland, who gave the keynote lecture but died suddenly less than a fortnight later.

The preface describes how the Irish-Scottish Academic Initiative (ISAI) was set up in 1995 linking three universities in Scotland and Ireland and spanning three subject areas: History, Celtic Studies/the Irish language/Scots Gaelic; and literature in the English language. The first major ISAI conference was hosted by the University of Strathclyde in September 1997, and a record of its proceedings was subsequently published as *Celebrating Columba* (Glasgow, 1998). In 1999 the initial institutional members – the University of Aberdeen, the University of Strathclyde, and Trinity College Dublin – were joined by Queen's University, Belfast.

This record of the second conference includes shortened versions of most of the plenary papers and summaries of contributions to seminar sessions, notably on language and literature, sport and culture, writing and film. It confirms the liveliness of the discussions generated by this fresh academic initiative. In itself it provides a valuable introduction and handbook. For the genealogist in Ireland, it serves as another timely reminder of the value of the links with Scotland over the years and particularly from the seventeenth century.

W. H. Crawford

C. W. Sullivan III (ed). *Fenian Diary. Denis Cashman on board the Hugoumont 1867-8.* Wolfhound Press, Dublin, 2001, pp.191.

The value of diaries as primary source evidence is widely-acknowledged. Their publication serves researchers in a number of areas in the fields of social, cultural and economic history and they are very useful contextual sources for family historians. However, diaries kept by emigrants on board their journeys to their new world are almost invariably disappointing as a source. By nature they tend to be pedestrian and lacking in fresh insight, their on-the-whole prosaic nature reflecting more the ordinariness rather than the excitement of the voyage. Charles Sullivan III's edition of the diary kept by his ancestor Denis Cashman on board the *Hugoumont* during its journey from Ireland to Australia September 1867-January 1868 is, however, intrinsically interesting because Cashman, a convicted Fenian who was being transported to Australia for involvement in the Fenian uprising 1866-7, was on the last Irish convict ship to be sent there, the first having set out from Cork in 1791.

Although it is the diary of a political exile its contents will have more interest for its account of the marine life observed from the ship, including a riveting description of the catching and landing on board of a shark; it contains the complete words of songs sung in the many concerts and evening gatherings that broke the boredom of the voyage and which Cashman took great care to transcribe and record.

As was the case with many transported Fenians, Cashman was released early and made his way to the United States where he was able to continue his journalistic work on the Boston *Pilot* where he was joined by some of his family whom he had had to leave behind in Ireland.

Charles Sullivan has followed this publication all the way through from discovery in family papers to publication. The outcome, which includes a useful Introduction, is a well-presented and not-too-fussily-edited labour of love which has gone some way to making this reviewer at least think better of diaries of emigrant voyages.

Trevor Parkhill

William E. Hogg. *Mills. The Millers and the Mills of Ireland of about 1850.* Dublin, 2000 edition, pp. 348 plus Appendices & Index. No price given.

William Hogg has been among the most dedicated of researchers over the period of thirty years as archivist and researcher of this review's professional life. He has continued to exude the same gentlemanly charm and abundant knowledge in equal proportions: in short, an archivist's delight.

Better than all of that is his knowledge of sources, borne of many hours of patient research. His Introduction would bring a gleam of satisfaction to those who peddle their lectures to many audiences throughout the country, when he says 'During a lecture given by an expert in genealogical matters a casual mention made of the existence of the Valuation Office Mill Books at National Archives, Dublin provided the spark necessary to set this mill research project in motion.'

Where there are no county Mill Books, Hogg has himself sought out the information in the Griffith's valuation for the same period, particularly the valuers' notebooks. The outcome is a thorough listing of all the mills in Ireland that are mentioned in that most indispensable of sources, Griffith's Valuation covering the period from the late 1840s to the mid-1860s. The information is arranged, within counties, by townland, name of miller, type of mill (whether it is flax, corn, spade, flour or beetling – there are also references to woollen mills, cutlery mills etc) and observations on the valuation, the times of year in operation and other distinguishing details that are of an all-round general interest as well as being important to the growing lobby concerned with the preservation of Ireland's industrial heritage.

A word of acknowledgement about the design of the book is also appropriate. The information garnered from the Mill and Valuation books is represented under a number of headings, all necessarily spread out across the page so that the information relating to one entry can be read on the same line, as it is in the original. To this end, the broader-than-usual format of the book works very well, as does the inclusion of pleasing and useful illustrations and diagrams extracted from these sources. The very fine collection of photographs of thirty-three mills, many of them reproduced in colour in the Appendices, are themselves testimony to the extensive travelling and *in situ* research undertaken by William Hogg. Added to his hours of consultation of the original sources, particularly the Valuation Mill Books and other appropriate records, this worthy volume will serve for years to come not only as a work of reference but as an example to others.

Trevor Parkhill

James G. Ryan, *Sources for Irish Family History. A Listing of Books and Articles on the History of Irish Families*. Flyleaf Books, 2001 pp. 180, £21 IR£16.54

This book does exactly what is says on the tin. It is, therefore, not a listing of manuscript or original sources, as might be deduced from the main title (the few references to archival sources are, unfortunately, somewhat out of date and therefore not entirely reliable, such as that on p. 17 for the Abercorn Papers in PRONI as 'DOD 623', a call number that has not been used for years). The sub-title is more reflective of what it is: a listing of books and articles on the history of Irish families.

The very short Introduction, which is really a Preface, says that 'the references cited are mainly accounts of particular family lines and vary from fond and emotional accounts of families and their ancestral homes to the dispassionate, well-researched and fully-documented family studies and pedigrees.' In effect, this appears to be a thorough trawl through historical journals, national, local and parochial, which have featured articles and items relating to families, their history and the sources that have been consulted in the course of the research.

For a book that will undoubtedly prove to have a regular value for researchers, it is perhaps appropriate to warn them about some characteristics of the presentation of information that do tend to grate. The titles of books and journals referred to are not given in italics; in fact there are no distinguishing marks between any of the information fields that include title, name of journal, author. Indeed, in the case of articles in journals, the author is not given so that, for example, the two latest and most authoritative contributions on the history of the Maguire family, by Terence McCarthy and W. A. Maguire in *Familia* and *Clogher Record* respectively, do not give the names of the authors. Still, at least *Familia* gets a mention, so it can't be all bad, though it is referred to only as *Familia*, not *Familia: Ulster Genealogical Review*.

Trevor Parkhill